KLAI JUBA
a r c h i t e c t s

To the memory of my mother and companion, Glenone Mary Bogle

The Architecture of Fumihiko Maki

Jennifer Taylor Space, City, Order and Making

with James Conner

Birkhäuser – Publishers for Architecture
Basel · Berlin · Boston

A CIP catalogue record for this book is available from the Library of Congress, Washington D.C., USA

Bibliographic information published by Die Deutsche Bibliothek
Die Deutsche Bibliothek lists this publication in the Deutsche Nationalbibliografie;
detailed bibliographic data is available in the internet at http://dnb.ddb.de.

Graphic design: Miriam Bussmann, Berlin

© 2003 Birkhäuser – Publishers for Architecture,
P.O. Box 133, CH-4010 Basel, Switzerland
A member of the BertelsmannSpringer Publishing Group
Printed on acid-free paper produced from chlorine-free pulp. TCF ∞
Printed in Germany
ISBN 3-7643-6697-4

9 8 7 6 5 4 3 2 1

www.birkhauser.ch

Contents

When you think about Fumihiko Maki, it is the same thing as thinking about what modernism is, and its impact. The reason for this is that while Fumihiko Maki is one of the most prominent modernists, he is also one of the most outspoken critics of modernism. However, the important point here is that he is one of the most outspoken critics of modernism *because* he is a modernist.

The most typical modernists are generally thought to be Le Corbusier and Mies van der Rohe. However, they use classical techniques when making presentations based on the principles of modernism. For example, they use platforms or rows of pillars, applying the principles of modernism to create a photogenic look that is easy for anyone to understand, but their designs are fixed and frozen. For them, modernism has the form of a crystallized object like a sculpture. Therefore, their designs may have classical beauty, but tend to lack in the inherent features of modernism, such as flexibility with respect to function, humility towards the user, and continuity and blend with the city and surrounding environment.

Fumihiko Maki criticises this type of modernism, saying that it is fixed in time. The reason for this is that first and foremost he is a modernist. This is why he advocates group form, and conceives of the city and architecture as equal and integrated. This is not a correction to modernism, but the true form and central value of modernism. When you compare Fumihiko Maki with Le Corbusier and Mies van der Rohe, they only seem to be architects that represent a mix of modernism and classic architecture.

Traditional architecture in Japan was flexible and urban in the past. In this respect, Fumihiko Maki is very Japanese. However, contemporary traditionalists in Japan are not flexible by comparison. There is no mistake that modernism and traditional Japanese architecture created Fumihiko Maki, but he was not satisfied to stay there. He continually criticises modernism, looking for its true form.

Fumihiko Maki is flexible, no matter which angle you look from. Therefore, the way he approaches architectural design is not frozen, and continues to change. The reason for this is that he continually pays close attention to each environment and has a respect for it. He does not forget to pay attention and have respect for the time that flows through that structure and the circumstances and time in which it exists. Since his designs continue to change, his architecture does not become old, and has an eternal life. Architecture is inherently a paradoxical art like this. And modernism is a paradoxical concept. Fumihiko Maki understands this paradox more deeply than anyone else.

Preface

I first met Fumihiko Maki when I visited Japan in 1975 as a Japan Foundation Fellow. He had kindly agreed to act as mentor for my study program on The Design and Use of Open Space in Contemporary Japan on the introduction of the renowned writer and historian Teiji Itoh who had started my interest in Japanese architecture and gardens with his lectures at the University of Washington in Seattle. From that time on I have been most fortunate to be under the care and guidance of Fumihiko Maki for my various research undertakings on gardens and current architecture in Japan. Over those twenty-seven years I have developed an appreciation and, I believe, an understanding of the architect and his work. The following pages draw on that understanding to present an interpretative and critical reading of the thinking, writing and designs of Fumihiko Maki from the 1960s to the present time. The book explores Maki's attitude to the shaping of space, relationships in form and place, the city, the concept of order, the role of technology and the handling of materials. It is concerned with the development and shifts in Maki's work with regard to his perception of place and time, and his architectural response to engage with, and communicate, these. Con-

sequently, Maki and his architecture are located against the background of Japanese society and culture and within the framework of modern architecture.

Rather than following a time sequence, the history is presented under a number of themes. These themes address dominant concerns of Maki's career: Space, City, Order and Making. For the most part, there are two essays on each theme, with the first essay addressing the major contributions of that aspect of his work in the early years, and the second essay more generally concerned with later material. The exception is the chapter on Making which fuses the two indivisible issues of Technology and Materials.

While there have been numerous publications on Maki, principally in architectural journals, to date there has been no overall account of his career. In 1997 Princeton Architectural Press published a selective retrospective book entitled *Fumihiko Maki: Buildings and Projects* that was structured as projects interspersed with invited essays. Prior to this, Serge Salat and Françoise Labbé presented an interesting book entitled *Fumihiko Maki: An Aesthetic of Fragmentation* in 1988, but it was limited to a specific period and concern.

My own library contains 526 references to Maki that contribute to the background for this book. This number of references (and mine are almost entirely in English) in themselves speak for the significance of Maki's architecture. In view of this, my wealth of material, knowledge of his buildings in Japan and elsewhere, and long association with Maki, suggested the possibility of this book. Over the years, research and writing associated with the production of this book provided material for the following conference presentations: "Maki and Movement Spaces", SAHANZ, Melbourne, 1998, "Strategy for Bigness: Maki and Group Form", ACSA International Conference, Rome, 1999, and "Movement Spaces and the Work of Fumihiko Maki", UIA, Beijing, 1999.

As with so many of my past writings, I was fortunate to have the very able and willing assistance of Susan Clarke, Senior Research Assistant at the Faculty of Architecture, University of Sydney. Without Sue helping me in the search and compilation of publications, keeping me and my material in order in her careful and exact manner, I would never have found my way through all the rich data written by Maki and numerous critics. As always, thank you Sue. Also my thanks to Jeanne Leppard of the School of Design and Built Environment, Queensland University of Technology, for her kind assistance in the final throes of handling the material. Thanks again to Susan Clarke for the first editing of the text, and to Felicity Shea in Brisbane for her most helpful advice and copy editing of the material before it left for Europe. Books are group exercises and so many people contribute to their production. In this case, Ria Stein of Birkhäuser Publishers was the key figure in her support for the book and her understanding of just the kind of book it wanted to be. My thanks also to Angelika Schnell for taking over the reins for a time when Ria had her new baby. Thank you Ria for returning to the task of steering the book with never-failing interest and enthusiasm through all of the later stages. At Birkhäuser, too, thank you to so many who did the polishing of the final product. I would especially like to acknowledge the elegant creativity of the book designer, Miriam Bussmann, who has made the book the artistic object that it has become. I send a very special vote of gratitude to Fumihiko Maki for his great generosity in providing the majority of the illustrations for this publication. I wish to particularly thank Kiwa Matsushita and Hiromi Kouda, in Maki's office, who extended such gracious assistance in the procurement of the illustrations for the book. Their patience and care throughout a long and demanding task and their clear presentation of the material earned my deep appreciation. Thank you.

The experience of the architecture, the long discussions with Maki and various associates and colleagues, would not have been possible without the support of the Japan Foundation, which, on two occasions, in 1975 and 1994, provided me with fellowships to visit Japan for extended periods. Also, I would especially like to thank Hiroshi Watanabe, Koichi Nagashima, Kengo Kuma, Hiroyuki Suzuki and Toshihiko Kimura for the insight they provided into Maki's work during long conversations. In addition, thank you to Kengo Kuma for his incisive Foreword to the text. To the members of the staff of the Maki office, my gratitude for accompanying me on visits to the buildings, and for providing excellent insight into the projects. In particular, I would like to thank Heather Cass, Roger Barrett, Mark Mulligan and Reiko Tomuro for informative discussions, great companionship, and lots of good fun on so many visits to Maki's buildings, whether completed, or, just as often, in construction.

But the most important person who aided me in the early years in Japan was my mother, Glenone Bogle, who lived with me in Tokyo and Kyoto and accompanied me on multiple extended trips (as she did in so many other countries), taking care of my two small children. She made it possible, and this book is dedicated to her.

On my later visits I was accompanied by James Conner, who was always there to help on all occasions. In particular, I would like to send him a special thanks for his major role in the collecting and cataloguing of the photographs. With this book he has been a true partner in every sense, giving marvellous support and encouragement in every possible way.

Finally I would like to say thank you to Fumihiko Maki for his friendship, and for his warmhearted and ever bountiful guidance and support over very many years.

1 Fumihiko Maki

Fumihiko Maki has stated that "architecture must not only express its time but survive it."[1] Within this sentence lie clues to Maki's central visions of architecture. First, there is the obligation of architecture to be the bearer and transmitter of culture. In this role architecture responds to and reflects its time. Second, there is the need for architecture to surmount the conditions of its time and embody eternal messages having to do with both physical and spiritual habitation. These beliefs echo throughout his writing, teaching and designs. In more particular respects one can observe Maki's innate sense of form and space, the unfailing judgement of his eye, his sensitivity in the use of contemporary materials, his command of the architectural detail, and his natural grasp of technology and the art of building.

Outside the mainstream, Japan held a fringe avant-garde position in the development of modern architecture for much of the second half of the twentieth century. The dramatic sculptural concrete buildings of Kenzo Tange and Kunio Mayekawa and the visionary imagery of the Metabolists drew attention to Japanese architecture in the 1960s. Of this Maki was a part, as he shared the tendency of the following decades for avant-garde designers in Japan to move towards refinement and elegance in new work. By the 1980s and 1990s, Japanese architecture had moved again into a central leadership position, drawing world recognition through the progressive theories and writings of architects such as Maki, Arata Isozaki and Toyo Ito. So in the genealogy of Japanese architecture Maki stands in succession to Makekawa and Murano (who he greatly admires), was a short-time pupil of Kenzo Tange, and shares the next generation with the other Metabolists, such as Kishio Kurakawa and Kiyonori Kikitake. While Isozaki and Ito are younger men, their work can be seen to run parallel to Maki's later career during what continues to be a peak in Japanese design, with the international acknowledgement of the leadership position of Japanese architects in providing meaningful expression to the electronic world.

Within an often-shifting context Maki stood fast by the principles of the Modern Movement. Maki is aware of its shortcomings and sought to extend its capabilities through an acknowledgement and accommodation of complexity and through enhanced imagery. At heart Maki is an urbanist and his urban theories are among his most significant contributions. The buildings are intensely urban in space and spirit, inspired by and generated in form and surface, as responses to the general and specific contexts of the city. To Maki, urban design is an art of communication concerned with and expressed through the shaping and structuring of physical and social space. Today, Maki is among the most celebrated architects of modern architecture in the world forum and in his native Japan.[2] Remarkable is the extraordinary scope of his contributions, embracing his teaching and extensive writings, along with the broad canvas of his architectural designs, ranging from small buildings to very large structures.

The fact that Maki was born and grew up in Tokyo in the Kansai region of Japan whereas many of his colleagues came to Tokyo as students from other places, has a significance clearly evident to a Japanese but not readily comprehended from an outside position. The various regions of Japan have their own codes and modes of behaviour, and a son of the Kansai is distinct and recognisable. This partially explains much about Maki's ethics and conservative manner. Maki is an international and cosmopolitan figure, having studied in the United States and travelled, lectured and built throughout much of the world. He is highly informed, and equally relaxed and at home in local and international arenas. His strong Renaissance attributes are masked behind his slight build and modest demeanour. There is a depth of both Japanese and Western history underlying the conception of the work, and playful references sometimes surface where least expected. Maki is the inheritor of the Japanese capacity to operate comfortably in contradictory situations, blending the traditional spirit with advanced technologies and happily combining conservatism with the most radically modern views. His special position within diverse cultures provides him with a unique perspective, which allows him to derive a certain perception from Western rationalism but to enrich it with the sensitivity of his inherited background. The smooth blending of traditions in Maki's architecture produces a richness that tempers the harsher aspects of today's global innovations. The work retains a sense of local place and tradition, and a transference of human sentience, despite the universal and contemporary nature of the materials and technologies that he uses. It manages to represent that which is local and human through that which is global and technological. This he achieves through a language of abstraction, using the tectonics of architecture as his tools.

Maki is the consummate professional. He is the pivotal figure in a smoothly running office to which clients return, often many times over. He is a man of great energy, who never seems busy and rarely becomes ruffled. He gives undivided attention to whoever or whatever the matter is at hand, and his clear, uncluttered desk tells of his meticulous way of working. His productivity, of vast quantity and quality, in his writing and building continues unabated. This extensive output comes from his medium-sized office which operates as the nerve center for the numerous site offices which extend and apply the creativity on the building site in collaboration with crafts people and builders. Until 1997, when he designed an office for himself as part of the Hillside West complex, Maki practiced from the design office in Nihonbashi, Tokyo, that he had established when he first set up his practice in Tokyo on his return in the 1960s from studying and teaching in America. The site office is a major component in the working structure of the Japanese construction industry, as many key decisions are made during the progress of the job, some in quite late stages of completion. Maki differentiates clearly between the intent and the responsibility of different work places, as he states that "the atelier must protect and maintain an intellectual world that transcends reality" and "the field office is not only the place for the liberation of the work of architecture from the world of thought – it is where one first learns how formidable the task of creation truly is."[3] Maki's field offices are now scattered throughout the northern hemisphere and he regularly travels to Europe and America to supervise his various overseas projects.

While mostly known for his buildings and urban proposals, Maki is a renowned educator, having taught at Washington University and at Harvard's Graduate School of Design in America and having served as Professor of Architecture at Tokyo University. In addition, he has been invited as a visiting professor to many universities throughout the world. His built work is informed by his scholarly pursuits in architectural and urban theory. These have been published in the form of design projects, reports and essays in journals, booklets and books. These extensive writings have had a marked impact on a broad range of design theory, marking Maki as a theorist of significance. Maki is fluent in the English language, and a considerable number of his publications have appeared in both Japanese and English.[4] His use of words is poetic, and the language in which his thoughts are expressed has an eloquence akin to that of Louis Sullivan, Aldo van Eyck or Louis Kahn. The explicit theories in the writings become manifest as implicit theories in the built works. This intellectual, intelligent and critical foundation underlying his architecture imparts a certain rigour and conviction to the buildings. Maki's words are as creative as his drawings.

Words and historical precedents are tools fully deployed to assist, identify and formulate the approach and solution. Research into the architectural, technological and cultural context preceding and surrounding the project is critical to the emergence of the design. The language is freely based, resulting in an eclectic permissiveness.

The drawing content of the creative act begins with the first line on a piece of paper. In an essay "The Life of a Drawing", he writes of the act of design, stating that "the single line of a drawing eventually begins to control and influence the movement and the way of life of tens of thousands of people. It is perhaps the most romantic act of brute force possible."[5] He works loosely, often in a gridded notebook, with a series of sketches. The sketch is a highly valued part of the process, it is "appealing precisely because it records a dream that will not be fulfilled."[6] But the initial image in the sketches is not something with presence and tangible form, but rather a "spatial entity" that later evolves into the design.[7] He works with space and form and accommodates specific functional needs within the developed overall concept. So "in the early stages of design the desired spatial entity is conceived and manipulated", then consideration is given to the detailed design conditions so as "to reorganise the required items to see if they can be accommodated in the desired spatial domain".[8] Maki does not see himself as a radical designer; rather, he says "I still compose."[9] Much of Maki's composing is determined by the eye, working with drawings and the numerous form and structural models produced at all stages of the process. The computer fills many design roles in the office, notably for exploring possibilities and generating new and complex forms, but this does not replace hand drawing which, for Maki, provides a special field for inspiration and development, as "one sketches not only to give expression to forms and ideas that are already developed or that have just come to mind, but to call forth new forms and ideas."[10] In writing of advances in computer technology Maki concludes that, in considering the processes and the work of making, "we realise that we still rely on the set of three independent operations, thinking, making judgements and using one's hands − that humans have used for thousands of years."[11]

Notes

1 Fumihiko Maki, "City image, materiality" in Serge Salat & Françoise Labbé (eds.), *Fumihiko Maki: An Aesthetic of Fragmentation,* New York, Rizzoli, 1988, p. 15.

2 Among his numerous awards are the Pritzker Architecture Prize and the Gold Medal of the International Union of Architects.

3 Fumihiko Maki, "Field office", *Fumihiko Maki: A Presence Called Architecture – Report from the Site,* Gallery Ma Books, Catalogue for an exhibition for Gallery Ma, Tokyo, TOTO Shuppan, 1996, p. 37.

4 Many of Maki's essays in Japanese have been translated into English by Hiroshi Watanabe, in a sympathetic manner that retains the meaning and eloquence of the original texts.

5 Fumihiko Maki, "The life of a drawing", *Selected Passages on the City and Architecture,* internal publication of Maki and Associates, Tokyo, 2000, p. 15.

6 Maki, "The life of a drawing", p. 16.

7 Maki, "The life of a drawing", p. 16.

8 Fumihiko Maki, "Space, image and materiality", *The Japan Architect,* 16, Special Issue on Fumihiko Maki, Winter 1994, p. 8.

9 Conversation with Maki, Tokyo, 1995.

10 Maki, "Space, image and materiality", p. 6.

11 Maki, "Field office", p. 37.

Form diagrams from "Notes on collective form".

2 Space: Space and Group Form

An understanding of the nature of space and time, and consequently the nature of the particular definition of space and time in architecture, evolves out of the knowledge, beliefs, technologies and needs of particular cultures. Changes in any of these will alter the political, social, functional and aesthetic factors that temper the demarcation of space. Japan in the twentieth century is clearly demonstrative of such shifts, which are then reflected in social and political space.

Constructs of space and their exploration through time have been constant preoccupations of Maki's throughout his career, from the Golgi structures of the 1960s to the enveloping cathedral-like volumes of the gymnasiums and exhibition buildings of the 1980s and 1990s. In his early architectural projects and writings, Maki addressed major issues that remain central to contemporary urban theory. Critical among these are the necessity to provide loose urban spaces responsive to the fluctuating needs of contemporary society, and to design environments that, despite the restless nature of the urban setting, engender a sense of communion and communication between the individual and the place created.

Maki prioritises the satisfaction of social need and the generation of space over technical possibility, as he writes that "the new kinds of spatial relationships modern technology has produced in the built environment were created for reasons other than that they have merely become technically possible."[1] Consequently, the designs derive directly from the generation of interior space. He states, "I would have the forms of interior spaces determine what the parts are, establish relationships of parts, and develop and mould the image of the whole."[2] Such an approach to design is in accord with his modernist position. In Maki's architecture, however, the precedence given to interior space over exterior appearance, and the very nature of the arrangement and connection of the functionally generated spaces, would seem also to be descended from the compositional techniques common in Japan since the feudal period, which are based on the linkage of individually conceived units of space.

Historically, Maki's work demonstrates the evolution of his perception and position regarding appropriate spatial marks, paths and envelopes, which are responsive to the conditions and needs of the particular circumstances. These spatial elements also reveal his broad concerns, and propose remedies for situations beyond those specific to the individual buildings. Despite his sensitivity to today's dominance of time and speed over space, one finds a consciousness that the accommodation of the dimension of the human body in space is the central responsibility of architecture. Maki's architecture, given its temporal as well as spatial determination, has always been appropriately attuned to respond to new needs. Further, with a firm foundation in both Japanese and Western understandings of space, Maki has been strategically placed to evolve new patterns of spatial division and enclosure, accommodating emerging global perspectives on representation, possession and protection. The grounding of his think-ing on space derives from his upbringing in Japan, his experience

Yoshiro Taniguchi, Sasaki House, Tokyo, 1937.

and education in America, and the broadening of his perspectives with travel. The genesis of his awareness of, and responsiveness to, the commensurate nature of social and spatial need is to be found in his projects of the 1960s. This concern persists throughout his career as he claims, "We are the generators of new forms to accommodate new spaces which can respond to social needs. It is not the form that responds to social need, but the space."[3]

Background

Since he was born in 1928, Maki's childhood and youth were spent prior to, during and immediately after World War II. During this period he had an uncommon upbringing which provided an early introduction to both Japanese and Western expressions of space. On the one hand he enjoyed the daily experience of the complex city of Tokyo, and on the other, due to the privileged position of his family, he was exposed to some of the most modern architecture and art in the country.

Maki's childhood Tokyo strongly conditioned his thinking and provided a lasting basis for his spatial constructs in architecture. He developed an acute consciousness of the general morphology and spatial sequences of the old city streets in the territory of his early years. Memorable too were his impressions of the rambling traditional houses of his friends, and his school in Tokyo, Yoshiro Taniguchi's Keio Hiyoshi Primary School, with its "constantly changing spaces, terraces, and mysterious corners for hiding".[4] Maki draws parallels between the spaces of his primary school and the city of Tokyo which "is a great gathering place made up of many small informal places".[5] It is from such experiences that Maki developed an early sensitivity to the conceptual structure of space.

Maki's visits to modern houses provided a most uncommon experience for a young boy in Japan in the 1930s. He mentions the Kameki Tsuchiura House, 1937, designed by an apprentice of Wright's, and Yoshiro Taniguchi's Sasaki House, 1935, commissioned by an uncle of Maki's.[6] In addition, Maki was aware of other radical examples of modern architecture, such as the houses of Sutemi Horiguchi and Antonin Raymond, and through his family's interests he became aware of leading movements in the Western arts. Further images were formed by his visits to the new ships in the harbour – images which, from an early age, he associated with the modern house.[7] Maki recalls the deep and lasting impression made on him at the time by their starkly different designs, and he acknowledges their continuing influence on his thinking.

While the post-war rebuilding of Japanese cities was impressive in its speed, both housing and the public areas of the cities were spatially inadequate. Space, in every sense, was at a premium. Expectations about social and political space within Japan differ widely from those of the Western world, as do the actually lived experiences of physical space. By 1975 living patterns had become such that workers commuted vast distances to an affordable dwelling unit that averaged 5.1 mats (8.4 square meters) per person. Traffic jams blocked the streets, and 22,000,000 passengers travelled on public transport in Tokyo per day, with loading at three hundred per cent above capacity.[8] Further, following World War II with the increase in Western, notably American, influence, there was an undermining of the old supportive social structure with its strict but clear definitions of place, resulting in social confusion and disorientation. It seemed that, to survive, society and the new city demanded radically different spatial organisations.

Maki's period of architectural education in the Department of Architecture (Faculty of Engineering) at the University of Tokyo, from 1948 to 1952, provided a further duality of awareness of the Japanese and Western comprehension and experience of space. At the University and in Kenzo Tange's atelier, where he studied for three months after graduation, Maki was further exposed to the quite alien Western view of space. He learnt of the modern understandings and representations of continuous and enveloping space as explored in Cubism, and architecturally embodied in the open plan and the horizontal window. Frank Lloyd Wright's Imperial Hotel in Tokyo was a familiar icon and published works of Le Corbusier and Mies van der Rohe were available for study.[9] In coming to terms with these concepts Japanese architects came to see the ideal modern city of the new age as unfettered, open-ended and spatially continuous. Tokyo provided the reality of space in the post-war recovery years in Japan, while at the University Maki studied the urban utopias of modern European design. The space problems of the Japanese cities and the grand schemes of redemption were brought together in the 1960s in the visionary proposals of Tange and his past students, such as Maki.

Following completion of his studies in Tokyo, Maki partly led a double existence on both sides of the Pacific. He furthered his education in mainstream modern architecture initially as a student at the Cranbrook Academy of Art, where he received a Master of Architecture degree in 1953, and for a year at the Graduate School of Design, Harvard University, where he obtained a further Master of Architecture degree in 1954. Important influences here were the campus buildings and spaces at Cranbrook, designed by Eliel Saarinen during his term as Director of the school, and the teachings of Josep Lluís Sert, then Chairman of the Harvard's Department of Architecture and Dean of the Graduate School of Design. Also of significance for Maki's increasing familiarity with the dynamic of modernist space were Sigfried Giedion's lectures on the space/time relationships of modern architecture, and certainly the essays in his book, *Space Time and Architecture*.[10] The humanities department at Harvard was particularly strong at that time, with many European scholars such as Giedion and Eduard Sekler having moved there in the post-war years. Also informing Maki's consciousness of Western notions of space was his time spent in the offices of Skidmore Owings and Merrill (1954–55) and Sert (1955–56). Maki then taught as Assistant Professor, 1956–58, and Associate Professor, 1960–62, at Washington University, St Louis, and at Harvard University, 1962–65. So Maki spent many years in America at a formative time of his

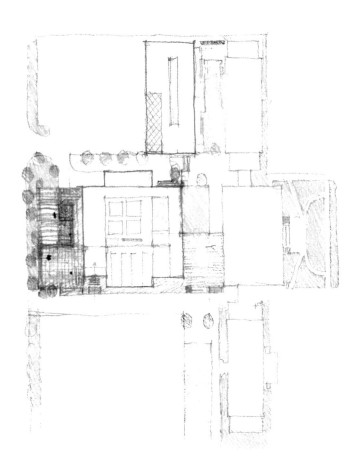

Visual Arts and Design Center, Washington University, St Louis, 2005. Plan.

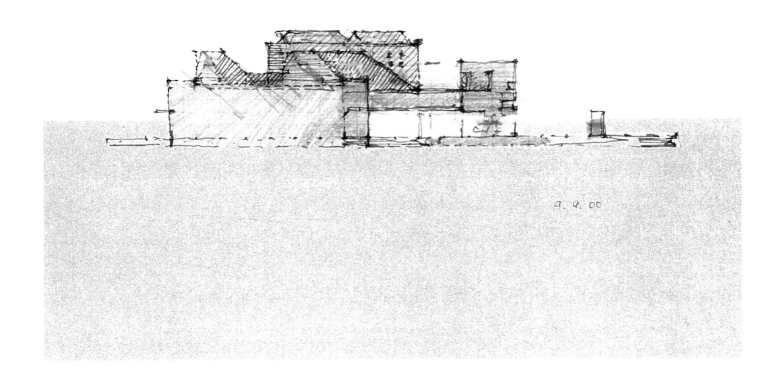

Visual Arts and Design Center, Washington University, St Louis, 2005. Elevational sketch.

Clustering village of the Mediterranean, Hydra.

career, thus reinforcing his early exposure to Western thinking and the arts previously made available to him in Tokyo.

At this time Maki was also given the opportunity to explore his developing ideas on space and form in a built structure. In 1957, in his role as a designer with the Washington University planning office, Maki designed the Steinberg Arts Center as a multi-purpose building for the library, art gallery and administrative offices. The result was a classically balanced concrete building with an over-sailing upper level supported by the lower volume, which, in turn, stood on a clearly demarcated podium. The building is currently being extended by Maki as a part of the Visual Arts Design Center for the University.

As a Graham Foundation Fellow (1958–60) Maki travelled in South-East Asia, the Middle East and Europe, widening his grasp of the fundamentals of architecture.[11] It appears that a dominant influence on his thinking was an increasing consciousness of the definition of exterior space by built form, and the power that architectural objects could exercise on each other across space and on space itself. Concurrent with his overseas experiences of the 1950s, Maki became involved in the Metabolist group which was evolving biologi-

cal and social theories on urban growth. The group consisted of young architectural graduates Noriaki Kurokawa, Kiyonori Kikutake and Masato Ohtaka, and the critic Noboru Kawazoe. A later graduate from Tange's atelier, Arata Isozaki designed related visionary work, but, like Tange, was never a member of the Metabolist group.

Maki contributed to the Metabolists' discussions and publications, but, because of his frequent absences in America, his involvement was never as close as that of, say, Kikutake or Kurokawa. However, due to his postgraduate American education and experience, Maki was able to contribute his familiarity with some of the most avant-garde ideas of the time to the deliberations of the group, and subsequently to Japan in general. These included the spatial and structural theories of Louis Kahn and the proposals of Team X and other complementary European movements, such as that based around Yona Friedman in Paris. In this role Maki made one of his most significant contributions to Japanese architecture in the 1960s and 1970s.

Early concepts: group form

Maki's early writings and projects reveal a blending of conceptual and applied theory.

The theoretical writings were supported by conceptual proposals as to how they might be brought to fruition in built form. These in turn were tested in built work and frankly assessed as to their success or failure by Maki or his associates.

At the same time as his involvement with the Metabolists, Maki taught urban studies in America and his ideas on urbanism were elaborated and more fully illustrated in a book with Jerry Goldberg, *Investigations in Collective Form,* and, with Ohtaka, as "Some thoughts on collective form" in György Kepes's *Structure in Art and in Science,* 1965.[12] The study was described as an investigation of the morphological resultants of forces present in cities. The possible ordering means discussed were "compositional form", as understood in its conventional sense, "megaform" and "group form". His thinking towards collective form had evolved from his reading of the traditional village patterns in Japan, and from his travels with the Graham Foundation Fellowship when he formed strong impressions of the informal cohesion of vernacular settlements such as Italian hilltowns. The lessons ranged from those available in the intimate clustering of small villages, as found along the Mediterranean, representing what he called group

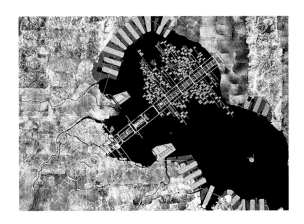

Kenzo Tange, Tokyo Bay Proposal, Tokyo plan, 1960.

Original "master-plan" for Hillside Terraces, 1967.

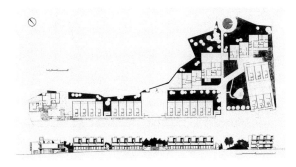

form, to the dominance of vast space by memorable objects as with Le Corbusier's government buildings at Chandigarh, representing megaform.[13] He wrote of the small villages, "the community, the collective form, was composed of quite simple spatial elements such as rooms arranged around a small courtyard ... I saw in those collective forms an expression of regional culture."[14] He was to conclude that "group form" was found to arise from the people themselves, while "megaform" was associated with power.

In *Investigations in Collective Form* Maki makes the first written use of the word "mega-structure", though Banham suggests (and Maki agrees) that the term may have been in usage in discussions in American schools when Maki was teaching there.[15] Maki defined a mega-structure as "a large frame in which all the functions of a city or part of a city are housed. It has been made possible by present-day technology. In a sense it is a man-made feature of the landscape. It is like the great hill on which Italian towns were built."[16] Clearly, Le Corbusier's Project A for Algiers contains the seeds of such a structure. Maki identifies the mega-structure as presenting one of three possibilities for ordering the city, and draws upon Tange's Tokyo Bay Proposal,

1960, as an illustration. Although Maki regarded the importance of the mega-structure as a new concept, he eventually rejected it as unsuitable on the basis of the permanent nature of its massive presence in the context of change. He leant clearly in favour of "group form".

Maki's group form was derived as a formal/spatial strategy for organising physical fabrics, urban and rural, large and small. His exploration of group form as a means of handling large and complex assemblages and units evolved through projects such as the proposal for Shinjuku, 1960, Rissho University, 1968, and the Hillside Terraces, 1969, to the large "cloud" complexes, including the gymnasiums and exhibition buildings of the 1990s. These projects seek to humanise bigness, when bigness is inherent in the program. The designs are based on a policy of accepting and accommodating the large by means of strategies of uncontainment and incompleteness. Maki's group form provides for an overriding cohesiveness brought about by the amalgamation of loose parts linked by revealing clues of relationships to provide a sensed, rather than a material, order. The entity retains a fluctuating ambiguity with a shifting focus from the whole to the part and

back again. The conceptual openness of the compositions provides for multiple penetrations and an acceptance of and responsiveness to uncertainty.

Maki's theories on group form derive from ways of thought that embrace the incomplete, the unpredictable and the transient, and suggest ways by which the current urban condition, with its demands and complexities, might well be addressed.

Group form 1960s

In their essay "Toward group form", which appeared in the 1960 book *Metabolism: The Proposals for New Urbanism*[17] Maki and Ohtaka first clearly delineated the intentions and means of achieving "group form", in which a number of elements compose an ensemble by virtue of a system inherent in each element.

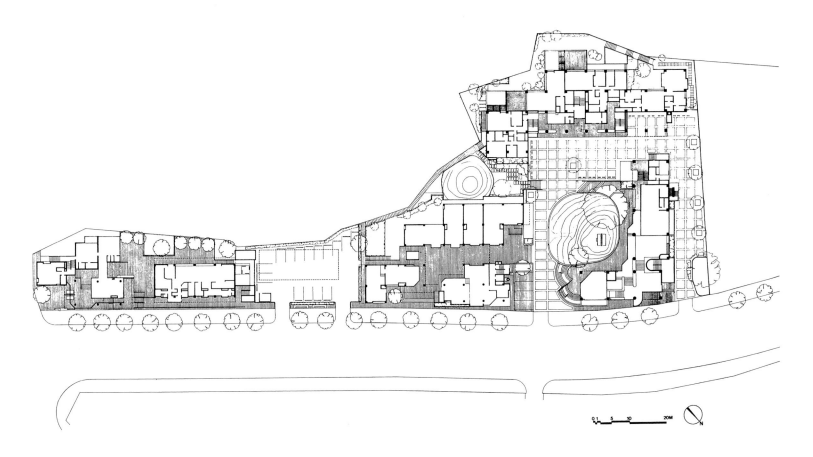

Plan: result of the "master-program" for Hillside Terraces.

Group form developed as a critique of the static nature of "master planning" and its demonstrated inability to grapple with the problems of the cities. Cities which were described by Maki and Ohtaka as being either confused or monotonous, lacking elasticity and flexibility, and incapable of visually accommodating the super-human scale of modern systems and units.[18] The basic intention of group form planning was to provide for the individual and the collective within a rapidly changing context, giving expression to the particular (including the region) and the general. "Collective form is, however, not a collection of unrelated, separate buildings, but of buildings that have reasons to be together."[19]

For the "master-plan" they substituted the "master-program", which was conceived as involving a temporal dimension. The passage from "plan" to "program" is evident in the design for the Hillside Terraces, for which Maki had first designed a "master-plan" which was considered too static to work in reality. They described "master-design" as "a formative technique, as an indicator and evaluator of intentions, and if possible as a tool for the generation of collective form".[20] The key lies in the possibility of open-ended and evolving planning. The term "master-form" was also introduced as an "ideal" which "can move into ever-new states of equilibrium and yet maintain visual consistency and a sense of continuing order in the long run ... The vital image of *Group form* derives from a dynamic equilibrium of generative elements, not a composition of stylised and finished objects."[21] The equilibrium of "master-form" was to be sustained by the elements present at any given time. In a perceptive article of 1976, Heather Cass identified in "Toward group form" the attempt "to reconcile the deterministic object-oriented tradition of the West with the indeterminate evolution-orientated tradition of Japan".[22]

Shinjuku Station Project

The Shinjuku project is clearly illustrative of "group-form" and "master-form" thinking. It was conceived as a total urban group embracing the smaller groupings of the shopping complex, office precinct and entertainment center, all raised on an artificial platform.[23] Different ordering principles were applied to the groupings, each designed to maintain unity despite the addition and subtraction of individual parts. This project introduced an early use of metaphor to assist in the conception of the work. Elements and systems were developed according to themes reflecting the activity and energy of life. The metaphors pertaining to physical patterns, such as the "petal" imagery of the entertainment zone, were poetic and organic rather than mechanistic. The entertainment zone serves as a good example of the "dynamic equilibrium" of the concept, wherein, like the petals of a flower, single or multiple elements (petals) can be taken away or added without destroying the evident governing structure of the object in its totality. The essential basis to this thinking can be found in a cultural understanding of the harmony possible from dynamic states of equilibrium and the beauty of imperfection, reflecting the cultural balance of the interdependence and connectedness of all things. As Masataka Ogawa wrote in 1973, "Maki's interpretation of the relationship between system and element denies existing ideas of architecture as an element and affirms the concept of architecture as an assemblage of elements. In terms of group concept, Maki's philosophy enables both the city and architecture to share a common, flowing life."[24]

The thinking that led to Maki's publications of 1960 and 1964 has remained consistent throughout his career. Although he later wrote that he should have paid more attention in the early schemes to external space and connections, rather than concentrating on form, it is clear that the projects have been conceived as defining and involving spatial and tactical environments.[25] This awareness provides a key to Maki's formal/spatial strategy wherein external space or space "between" is an implied linkage. Although structuralism in general, and the theories of Team X in particular, shared Maki's interest in designing flexible systems to accommodate choice and change, Maki's particular contribution through his various "group-form" proposals was unique in its easy acceptance of the incomplete.

The basic intentions and strategies of group form were laid down in the work of the 1960s, but variations on the themes are seen in the projects of the following decades. Of interest are "sequential group form" whereby the group form logic is sustained in a grouping emerging over time, and "cluster group form", which has a hen-and-chickens arrangement.

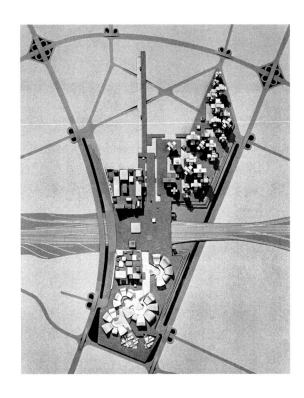

Shinjuku Station Project, Tokyo, 1960. Model.

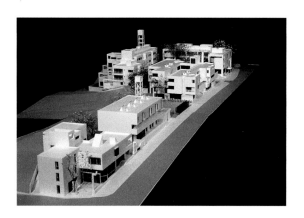

Hillside Terraces, Daikanyama District, Tokyo. Model.

Sequential group form

By the end of the 1960s Maki felt the frustration of attempting to achieve the unachievable in large-scale projects. He proposed a melding of well-designed "small parts" that would give rise to a city of parts dynamically evolving in an ever-shifting whole: the city viewed as a total collection of group form. It was with the Hillside Terraces that Maki hoped to first demonstrate his new approach to the design of the city.

Hillside Terraces (1967–98)

The Hillside Terraces project, which continued to grow after the commissioning of the first increment in 1967, provides a remarkable example of this theory within Maki's own oeuvre. The Hillside Terraces stretch down both sides of a fashionable street of the Daikanyama district of Tokyo.[26] This extensive project has been gently modified and finely tuned over time. The development is an ongoing private commission primarily of mixed residential and commercial and cultural uses, responding with each new addition to the changing structure and significance of the street, to the lessons learnt from the preceding segments, to the changing spirit and possibilities of

architecture, and to the developing ideas of its designer. In all, it is a remarkable example of consistency and diversity in an orchestration of forms and activities that (like the flower/petal analogy of the Shinjuku Station project) in each complete/incomplete stage remain suggestive of some governing structure. This is group form at its most dynamic, growing and evolving organically over time.

Clustered group form 1980s–90s

The clusters of group form are found primarily in the very large urban interventions of the 1980s and 1990s. They tend to be physically delineated as distinct from the city; the Tokyo Metropolitan Gymnasium, 1990, for example, is located both on and under a clearly defined podium. Yet there is a penetrability across the sites and around the forms that opens up the total grouping through spatial and temporal connections to the surroundings.

The majority of Maki's buildings prior to 1980 can be seen to derive spatially from linking compositions. However, after 1980 he was given commissions for two gymnasium complexes and a major exhibition hall and conference center and an international concert hall, all of which demanded many large single-vol-

ume spaces. These large buildings of the end of the century are characterised by a linking structure akin to that of his earlier, smaller buildings, composed with the principles of group form. The additional dimension added to this union was the dominance accorded to the main interior spaces. The principal volumes are vast cathedral-like caverns, brought low at the edges to give a sense of shelter. With the display of the ribs of the structures, the interior spaces take on a somewhat awesome medieval character. For these projects Maki divided the program into separate activities and provided individual spaces for the major components. These honorific single volumes are clearly differentiated by gleaming metal roofs. Models served in all cases to determine the volumes and the group form relationships. The mode of arrangement was established in the first of such groupings, the Fujisawa Gymnasium, 1984, where the main stadium and sub-arena were selected for special treatment. They, with the subsidiary volumes, were combined into asymmetrical groupings through working with the models to determine the compositions. Cohesion here is acquired through the drama of the large objects and the connections established with other minor, yet

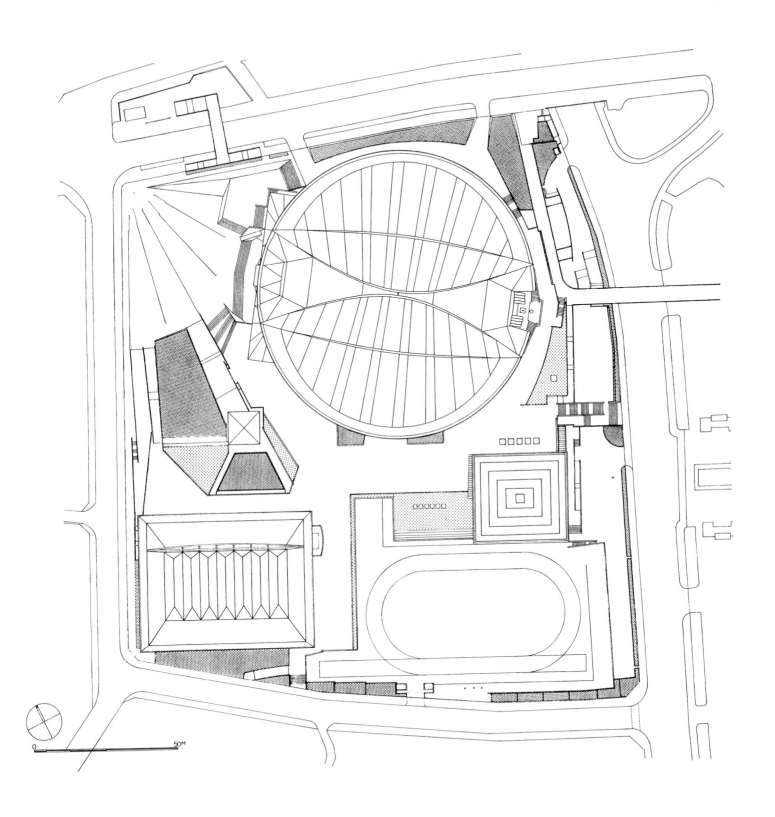

0   50M

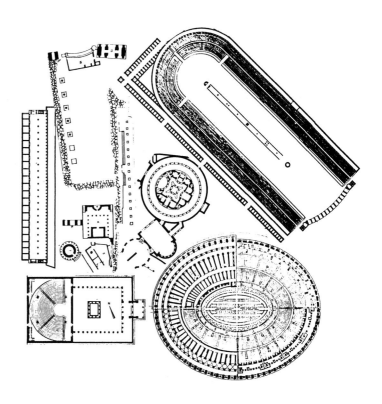

Maki's comparative sketch of early Roman stadia.

arresting, forms, commonly exploiting a mix of related and differing materials. The composition is determined not by direct kinship or subservience but by an adherence to individual presence and the overall sculptural relationship between the parts. The Fujisawa Gymnasium provided the precedent for the later large groupings of the Tokyo Gymnasium, Makuhari Messe, and the Kirishima Concert Hall.

In a city with little open space proportional to its population, the Tokyo Gymnasium makes a gesture by treating its entire site as an urban platform open at all hours. The distinctive roof forms of the various parts (the main arena, the small arena, the swimming pool and the entrance) penetrate and protrude above the raised podium and establish a dialogue across the site and hint of spaces and relationships below. Hence, on the podium the total composition is subtly linked across space in all dimensions. The heroic nature of the undertaking is underlined by Maki's drawing of a collage of early Roman stadia and halls that he sketched to show the thinking behind his own assemblage of forms. In such clusters, there is no sense of completeness of closure, but each group has its own open and balanced completeness. This is exemplified by the vast Makuhari Messe (Tokyo Exhibition Halls, Conference Center, Events Hall and other buildings), 1989, which in 1997 tolerated a further addition of vast dimension (18,000 square meters) without loosing the well-knit quality of the original group form.

The 1994 Kirishima Concert Hall in a dramatic mountain setting in Kagoshima province, Kyushu, provides a different example of

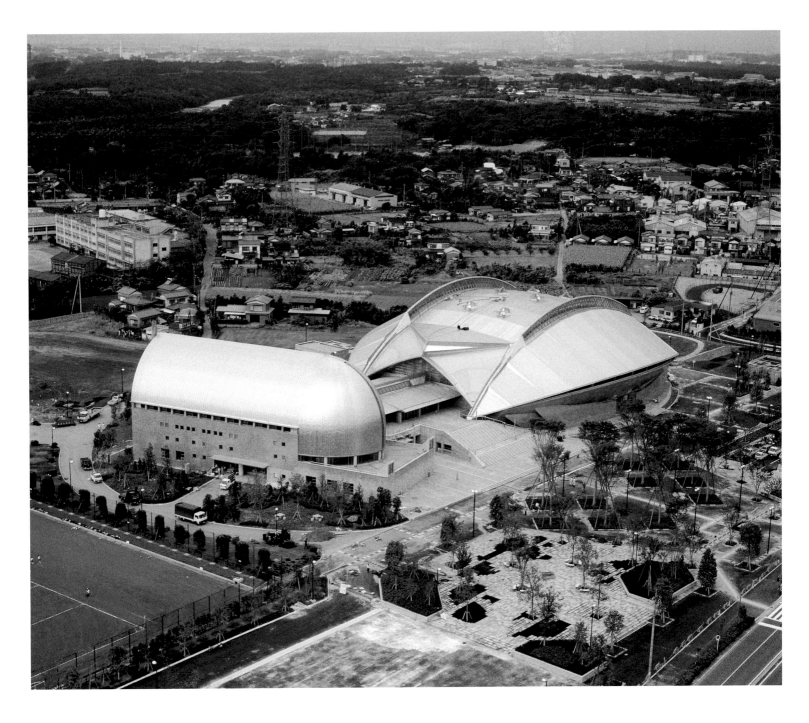

Fujisawa Gymnasium, Fujisawa, 1984.

Makuhari Messe, Stages I and II, Tokyo Bay, 1989.

cluster group form. There are three distinct parts to the complex: the two components of the main building consisting of the stainless-steel-roofed concert hall and a group of secondary performance spaces and practice rooms, and a third somewhat distant outdoor amphitheater located astride an axis at right angles to that of the Concert Hall. The outdoor stage faces a subtle and gentle space with grassed seating laid out in a semi-circle. The site planning has a marked kinship to the previous buildings in the "cloud" series, but distinct at Kirishima is the fleeing fragment, as the canopy of the outdoor theater appears adrift yet tied as if by taut violin strings to the

parent object. Triad, the Harmonic Drive Extension Complex, Hotaka, Nagano, 2002, is a group of buildings built for a company manufacturing precision instruments used on spaceships and cosmic telescopes. The complex consists of a loose but controlled, assemblage of three disparate parts: a laboratory, an art gallery and a guard house, held together in a subtle group form composition through the formal dialogue of the geometry of their disposition. It is a dynamic ensemble set in a rural landscape with a background of the Japan Alps. The composition opens with the simple rectangular mass of the guard house, seemingly lifted, with half its volume can-

Triad, Hotaka, Nagano, 2002.

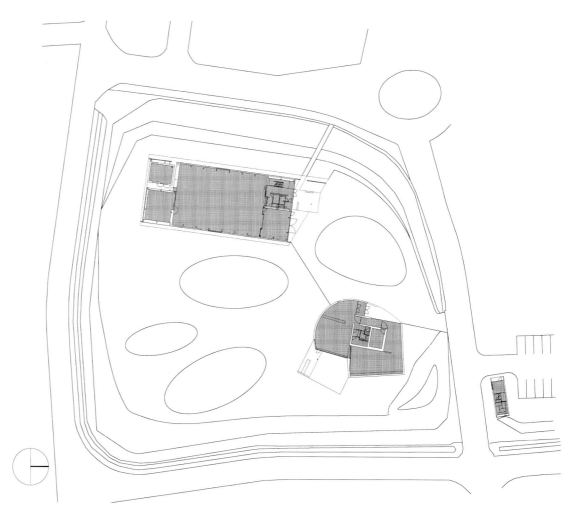

Triad, Hotaka, Nagano, 2002. Plan.

tilevered over the gentle slope. The research laboratory and the gallery enter into the formal relationship; the laboratory with its distinctive curved wall and roof vertically, and the gallery with a curved wall horizontally.

Looking back over Maki's early career it is evident that the mix of his background and training was unique, and that out of this he developed a particular vision. Further, Maki responded to the situation of the 1960s – the reality of post-war Japan and the social theorising of current European and American urban writings – with an acute concern for the social use of the city and the nature of the public urban realm. The key to meeting the needs of the city was seen by Maki to lie in the provision of spaces that responded through time to the shifting demands the city placed on them. Similarly, he believed that "spatial design must become a fountainhead of spontaneous, rich human events."[27] Maki's resulting strategy of "group form" is open-ended and operates in the dynamic of the unpredictable, as in the urban realm of today. It is a porous, adaptable system permitting change and penetration. As demonstrated in designs such as those for the Hillside Terraces, the principles of group form function across time as well as space. In addition, Maki's cross-cultural background encouraged an approach to design that evolved out of reciprocal exchanges between designer and circumstance, between activity and place.

Notes

1 Fumihiko Maki, *Selected Passages on the City and Architecture*, internal publication Maki and Associates, Tokyo, 2000, p. 18.

2 Fumihiko Maki, "An environmental approach to architecture", *The Japan Architect*, 48, 3 (195), March 1973, p. 21.

3 Conversation with Maki, Tokyo, 1995.

4 Maki, "An environmental approach to architecture", p. 20.

5 Maki, "An environmental approach to architecture", p. 20. The school is described by Maki as a "masterpiece" in Teijiro Muramatsu, "Humanity and architecture. Teijiro Muramatsu and leading Japanese architects. Dialogue Series 2: with Fumihiko Maki", *The Japan Architect*, 48, 9 (201), September 1973, p. 94.

6 Fumihiko Maki, "The present that is Tokyo", *Space Design*, 1 (256), January 1986, p. 140.

7 Maki talks of the importance of these experiences in Fumihiko Maki, "New directions in Modernism", *Space Design*, 1 (256), January 1986, pp. 6–7.

8 *An Administrative Perspective of Tokyo*, Tokyo, Tokyo Metropolitan Government, 1975.

9 The Imperial Hotel was quoted by Maki as the most successful example of ultimate dissolving of the partial units of space into a legible totality. Maki, "An environmental approach to architecture", p. 22.

10 Sigfried Giedion, *Space Time and Architecture*, Cambridge, Harvard University Press, 1941.

11 Maki discusses the impact of his travels under the Graham Foundation Fellowship in Fumihiko Maki, "Notes on collective form" (A new "Introductory chapter" to the reprint of material from the 1964 book of the same title), *The Japan Architect*, 16, Special Issue on Fumihiko Maki, Winter 1994, pp. 248–50.

12 Fumihiko Maki (in part with Jerry Goldberg), *Investigations in Collective Form*, St Louis, Washington University, 1964, and Fumihiko Maki and Masato Ohtaka, "Some thoughts on collective form", *Structure in Art and in Science*, ed. György Kepes, New York, George Braziller, 1965, p. 116–27, followed the original "Toward group form" published in English as *Metabolism: The Proposals for New Urbanism*. This material was also published in Japanese and illustrated by four studies, The Boston Study, Rissho University Campus, Golgi Structures, and the Senri New Town Civic Building. Further, Maki discussed this material in the office document of August 1967, entitled "Four studies in collective form – A summary". Maki considers this document to be of such significance in his work that it has appeared in a related text in several journals, the most recent of which is the reprint in the Special Issue on Maki in the *The Japan Architect*, Winter 1994, as "Notes on collective form".

13 Maki met Corbusier while visiting the site at Chandigarh.

14 Maki, "Notes on collective form", p. 248.

15 Reyner Banham, *Megastructure: Urban Futures of the Recent Past,* New York, Harper and Row, 1976, p. 70.

16 Maki, *Investigations in Collective Form,* p. 8.

17 K. Kikutake, N. Kawazoe, M. Ohtaka, F. Maki and N. Kurokawa, *Metabolism: The Proposals for New Urbanism,* Tokyo, Bijutsu Shuppansha, 1960.

18 Fumihiko Maki and Masato Ohtaka, "Toward group form", in *Metabolism: The Proposals for New Urbanism,* reprinted in Joan Ockman (ed.), *Architecture Culture 1943–1968,* New York, Rizzoli, 1993, pp. 321–24.

19 Maki, *Investigations in Collective Form,* p. 5.

20 Maki, *Investigations in Collective Form,* p. 7.

21 Fumihiko Maki quoted in, "The future of urban environment" in "Aesthetics and technology of pre-assembly", *Progressive Architecture,* 10 (45), October 1964, p. 178.

22 Heather Willson Cass, "Architecture as human experience," *Architectural Record,* 2 (160), August 1976, p. 78.

23 Under "News and comment", in November 1961 *The Japan Architect* (p. 8) reported that the Ministry of Construction had taken up the idea in the Maki-Ohtaka study for multi-storeyed blocks with floor space for "individually owned" flats and shops. "The idea was to create new 'ground' which could be divided up by small owners very much as the space along the street is now." However, while the Maki-Ohtaka study had advocated mixed use, the Government proposed to use the idea primarily for housing.

24 Masataka Ogawa, "Fumihiko Maki – Frontiers of contemporary Japanese art," *The Japan Architect,* 48, 3 (195), March 1973, p. 84.

25 Maki, "Notes on collective form", p. 250.

26 A further section, Hillside West, was completed in 1998 on a site a few hundred meters up the street from the earlier stages of the development.

27 Fumihiko Maki, "The theory of group form", *The Japan Architect,* 45, 2 (161), February 1970, p. 41.

Golgi Structures: Sketch.

3 City: Possibilities for Performance

The city has been the predominant focus of Maki's career since his student days, with the roots of a consistent urban theory already evident in his designs and writing of the 1960s. There is a mark of urbanity in all of Maki's architecture, including his country "villas", with buildings retaining a certain sophistication, and most exhibiting a detachment from the landscape. Independent of location, Maki's buildings are conceived as part of an urban whole. His writings have been dominated by investigations of urban form and by conceptual urban theory. For Maki, the collective city provides the rationale and stage for existence, and hence must be the primary focus in any architectural endeavour.

How to design the city to readily accommodate the change brought by the technologies and the volatile social structures of the new age has been an obsessive concern in Western architectural theory throughout the twentieth century. The proposals, ranging from the rigid, rationalistic designs of Ludwig Hilberseimer to the sprawling rural extravagance of Frank Lloyd Wright's Broadacre City, were based on the premise that the historic city was dead and that radical solutions of replacement had to be devised. For the Europeans this was to occur by clearing and rebuilding within the city, and in Wright's plan by going beyond it. Both models were implemented in part in the second half of the century in the city centers and suburbs of Europe, America and other advanced nations such as Australia, neither proving viable as a fitting model for twenty-first century urbanity.

The Japanese city bears little resemblance to the cities of Europe or America. Not only is it conceptually different in spatial organisation and use patterns, but the fundamental thinking of the Japanese about acceptable functional performance, appropriate spatial distribution, the definition of the public realm and aesthetic determinants, involves criteria at odds with Western theory.[1] Consequently, although modern architecture has been successfully absorbed into the Japanese city, urban planning theory sits uneasily, and for the most part has been rejected by the city itself. Large-scale implementations of European planning can be found only in new developments such as in Shinjuku in Tokyo and on the reclaimed land of the islands off Kobe. Generally, such attempts appear artificial and contextually contradictory. Exceptional is the axially planned city of Sapporo in Hokkaido.

Japanese cities, for the most part, are remarkably similar throughout the country,[2] and, while chaotic and aesthetically displeasing by conservative Western standards, they provide a safe, exciting and socially fulfilling environment attuned to the aspirations of the twenty-first century Japanese inhabitant. Further, the volatile, fluctuating patterns of conflict and discord that affect the visual reading of the city present a differing aesthetic embodying a new order and preference. With reference to the continuous rebuilding of the Japanese city, Yasufumi Kijima writes, "Indeed, changes in the built environment have become so radical that any resident of a Japanese neighbourhood will inevitably be

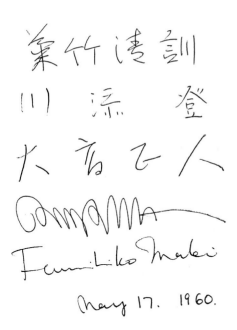

quite lost if he returns home after even the briefest absence of a few years."[3] So the urban problems confronted in Japan by the modern architect were quite distinct from those their colleagues elsewhere faced.

As a Tokyoite, Maki has a deep understanding and love of the city, and although his knowledge of Western cities informs his response to the Japanese situation, it is always tempered by an instinctive sense of the workings of the Japanese city. Maki has always designed with empathy towards the reality of the Japanese city, neither rejecting nor celebrating its vibrancy and dynamic tempo, but rather accepting its particular nature and working with it. Tokyo is the quintessential Japanese city, and for Maki it constantly serves as a reference.

Background

Maki's urban studies and the resulting urban theories need to be set against the mood prevailing in the profession in the 1960s when Team X's structuralist theories were propounded by the radical avant-garde of Europe. Further, Maki's early work has to be seen in the context of Japan in the post-war era when the search for a solution to the Japanese urban crisis was real and pressing: the situation seeming to demand radical urban intervention.

In the late 1940s, Japan was still classified by the United Nations as an "underdeveloped country"[4], and during Maki's youth the city of Tokyo was suffering from the results of the war and the beginning of the pollution caused by cars and the waste of industrial production. Immediately following the devastation of the bombing, Tokyo was rebuilt (still principally in timber) very quickly.[5] New planning controls were debated and implemented, but for the most part they were ineffective, appearing after much of the rebuilding had been completed. Consequently, the identifiable pattern of the old city of Edo which had survived in the plan of the pre-war city, re-emerged as the underlying structure of the new Tokyo. While the war and its aftermath had few direct physical consequences for Maki and his family, apart from the generally shared deprivations, the city, in its surviving past and in its emerging present, had a marked impact on the Maki's early thinking.

Metabolism:
the proposals for new urbanism

Given that during the time of urban rebuilding Maki was attending the University of Tokyo, it is not surprising that the emphasis of his projects was on rebuilding the city, and hence from his earliest formal studies Maki was working with the urban dimension. Students such as Maki who had contact with Tange were indoctrinated by his radical structuralist proposals, which provided the starting point for Metabolism. The structuralist vision derived originally from Le Corbusier, and later from the Team X manifestoes. In the late 1950s Tange became interested in this approach as applied to urban design, and accepted the opportunity to display his and other contemporary Japanese schemes when invited to the CIAM meeting at Otterloo.[6] The proposals of Japan's avant-garde applied such structuralist principles to the primary problem, which was the shortage of land: new sites had to be found, be they in the sky or over the sea.[7] These evolutionary notions of development were coupled with a quite advanced awareness of technological possibilities. In 1955 Konrad Wachsmann had lectured in Japan on the theories and applications of flexible, prefabricated systems. Being in America at the time, Maki had not attended the talks, but several of his colleagues had, and such ideas would have been in accord with the Japanese tradition of building.

Maki's concepts on adaptive planning were first given public voice in his contribu-

Summation plan from *Movement Systems in the City*, 1965.

tion, with Masato Ohtaka, to the Metabolist Group's publication *Metabolism: The Proposals for New Urbanism.* Five hundred copies of the publication were released, in English as well as Japanese, and made available for distribution at the World Design Conference held in Tokyo in May 1960.[8] This conference represented an exciting moment for Japanese architects, as it was the first international forum to be held in Japan since the war. The conference provided the first opportunity for the quite revolutionary ideas of the Japanese progressives to be heard by a large international audience. Tange presented his Boston Bay proposal, and the Metabolists leapt at the opportunity to put their ideas forward. Maki's and Ohtaka's presentations at the conference were less heroic than most, but they were

more directly practicable, presenting as they did a rational means of approaching the structuring of the city.[9] Further, the conference gave Japan's modernists their initial exposure to such international figures as Jean Prouvé and Paul Rudolph. Of particular interest to the Metabolist group was the presence of Louis Kahn, whose notion of "served" and "servant" spaces, and elevated movement networks and vehicular storage towers, had guided the development of their thinking. Also of importance was the input of the Smithsons, the highly vocal protagonists for the Team X proposals for new approaches to housing and urban development on structuralist principles. At the invitation of the Smithsons, Maki attended the 1960 Team X housing conference at Bagnols-sur-Cèze in the south of France,

making contact with many other members, including Giancarlo de Carlo. (Later at the Graduate School of Design at Harvard he was able to extend his familiarity with Team X's progressive views on city design through contact with Shadrach Woods, Jerzy Soltan, Aldo van Eyck and Jacob Bakema.)

The Metabolist manifesto in *Metabolism: The Proposals for New Urbanism* stated: "'Metabolism' is the name of the group in which each member proposes future designs of our coming world through his concrete designs and illustrations. We regard human society as a vital process – a continuous development from atom to nebula. The reason why we use such a biological word, the metabolism, is that, we believe, design and technology should be a denotation of human vitality.

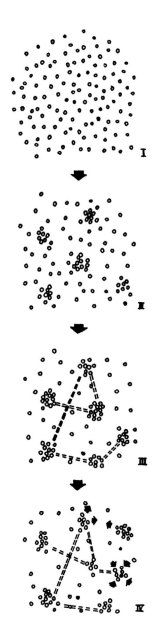

Node development structure from
Movement Systems in the City, 1965.

We are not going to accept the metabolism as a natural historical process, but we are trying to encourage active metabolic development of our society through our proposals."[10]

Generally, the essays in *Metabolism* present futuristic declarations, with Maki and Ohtaka's contribution proposing a rational, open-ended planning approach to accommodate the dynamics of the changing city. Their essay "Toward group form" first clearly delineated the intentions and means of achieving group form, and illustrated the concepts with the Shinjuku Station development proposal. These ideas were elaborated and more fully illustrated with other projects.[11] The issue contains three further illustrated essays, "Ocean City" by Kikutake, "Space City" by Kurokawa, and "Material and man" by Kawazoe. Maki's and Ohtaka's article appears

decidedly conservative given the somewhat radical tone of the document as a whole.

In *Metabolism* the Tokyo of the 1950s and 1960s is variously described. Kikutake writes, "Tokyo, a huge city, is worn out with bad sickness. She has lost proper control of [herself], because of her mammoth-like scale. ... The limitation of the horizontal city has far passed over from the ability of function and transportation and the living standard."[12] From Kurokawa comes the statement that Tokyo is "the biggest and most confused city [in] the world".[13] Elsewhere a graphic picture emerges from the report of Hursch in his 1965 book *Tokyo:* "Tokyo is a huge wilderness, a conglomerate mass of wooden cubes and concrete blocks, main arteries and narrow alleys, waterways and railbeds, of trees, cables and signs – a jungle crammed with people and filled with

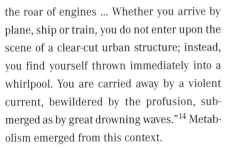
City room from *Movement Systems in the City,* 1965.

City corridor from *Movement Systems in the City,* 1965.

the roar of engines ... Whether you arrive by plane, ship or train, you do not enter upon the scene of a clear-cut urban structure; instead, you find yourself thrown immediately into a whirlpool. You are carried away by a violent current, bewildered by the profusion, submerged as by great drowning waves."[14] Metabolism emerged from this context.

The writings and schemes of the Metabolists were primarily concerned with determining new forms of urban order that would accept the conditions of a technically dominated world and lead to the revitalisation of the Japanese city. That is, change itself was seen to provide order. Chris Fawcett observed that the two radicals that are the roots of the verb for change in Japanese, *kawaru,* are transformations of the written sign representing motion and a simplification of the charac-

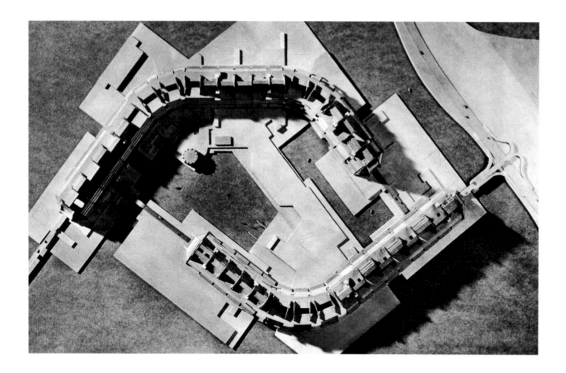

Kenzo Tange and MIT Students, study for Boston Harbour, 1959.

ter in *kanji* script that "expresses the idea of rearranging or disentangling something which is confused or tangled, and generally means 'to change'. In other words, 'change' is regarded as an organisational principle, not something disruptive and fickle."[15] Fawcett claimed that "it was this plateau of cultural agreement on which *Metabolism* was based, lending credibility to its vision of an environment as a sort of living plasma of demountable settings, a multi-strategy architecture of indeterminacy ... ."[16] Basically, the city would be regenerated by a continuous replacement of parts on a "metabolic cycle", as in nature. This is in accord with the Buddhist notion of the world-in-transformation where phenomena are viewed as transitory states rather than as fixed objects, which also ties closely with the Shinto vision of nature as a cycle of renewal. This thinking was compatible with the exist-

ing situation in the Japanese city, which constantly changes according to the natural patterns of decay and renewal. Further, this analogy is easily transferred to the individual building, where the Metabolist pattern of exchangeable and transferable parts sits well with Japanese traditional modular building practices. The frontispiece of *Metabolism: The Proposals for New Urbanism* depicted a swirling galaxy in infinite space proclaiming a visionary perspective.

The work of the Metabolist group (with Tange and Isozaki) was later shown in Tokyo in 1964, and drawings such as Isozaki's City in the Air, 1960, Kikutaki's Floating City, 1960, Kurokawa's Helicoids project, Helix City, 1961, and Maki's Golgi Structures, 1965, became the visionary symbols of the new spirit. Although the futuristic vigour and drama of the Metabolist proposals bear some comparison to the Archigram designs in England of

the same decade, the basic premise differs. Archigram drew primarily on a mechanistic metaphor, with accompanying notions of material impermanence that were British in their tectonic bases, whereas Metabolism, though technological in its elements, was inspired by biological growth. This orientation to evolving extensions and replacements of elements has its roots in a traditional understanding of the cyclical movement of death, decay and rebirth, one that is decidedly Japanese.

In 1963 the legal limit of building construction in Tokyo was lifted conditionally, opening up possibilities for the vertical proposals of the Metabolists. Their radical projects, which were to rescue Japanese cities from intense congestion and over-crowding through revolutionising the location and spatial structure of building units, reached but token form in such projects as Tange's Yamanashi Press and Broadcasting Building, Kofu, 1967, Kurokawa's Expo "Beautilion" Tower, 1970, and Nakagin Capsule Tower, Tokyo, 1972, and Kurokawa's parody of Kikutake's "Ocean City" in the Yamagata Hawaii Dreamland, 1967.[17]

The 1960 issue was the only publication of *Metabolism,* though its preface predicted ongoing participation and publications involving many contributors from different disciplines. Industry was interested in the concepts of prefabrication and exchangeable parts, and for a time there was cooperation across design and production, but Metabolism did not survive as a viable movement for long. The protagonists had always worked independently of one other and soon they drifted in different directions. Maki's shift in perception away from the technological ambitions for large-scale urban regrowth occurred quite early and was distinct.

It was, however, when Maki returned to Harvard in 1962 as Associate Professor at the Graduate School of Design that he was able to more fully formulate his new proposals for comprehensive urban investigations. At the same time he was working on a translation into Japanese of Paul and Percival Goodman's *Communitas,* which was published in Tokyo in 1967.[18] The mid-1960s were years of exploration for new means of structuring urban form. The primitive and vernacular were studied by, among others, Aldo van Eyck and Bernard Rudofsky, and lessons were drawn from the overall compositional strength of groups arising from the spontaneous gathering of similar and diverse parts, as in the vernacular village. Rudofsky's exhibition and accompanying book of 1964, *Architecture Without Architects,* opened a new perspective to jaded designers.[19] Certainly Maki drew on the Italian hilltown to illustrate his definition of "group form", and cites the Japanese village as a natural example of such an arrangement. In North America, J. B. Jackson was providing fresh visions of the roadside and the small-town vernacular; Marshall McLuhan was predicting a world dominated by media; and Buckminster Fuller was expounding on how to organise and build such a global city.

In this intellectual climate, in a studio project involving the Harvard 1963–64 class of Urban Design students, Maki explored the possibility of a new urban structure for Boston. It was published in 1965 as a study entitled *Movement Systems in the City,* following his *Investigations in Collective Form* of 1964.[20] This, in turn, was followed in 1970 by *What is Urban Space?* written jointly with Kawazoe Noboru.[21] The Harvard Boston study provides a remarkable contrast to the study for Boston Harbour prepared by Tange and students of the Massachusetts Institute of Technology in 1959. The Tange proposal involves two A-frame megastructure units supporting trays of housing units and bridging transportation and service channels. Maki's scheme, on the other hand, is strategic in intention rather than fixed and physical in form. The overall tenor of Maki's proposal for Boston involves a loose organisation based on connecting networks rather than on fixed physical planning: it is decidedly Japanese in its flexibility and the absence of clear visual order and control. A further urban study, "South Cove Infrastructure", which developed as a megastructure project, was undertaken by other students at Harvard, including Koichi Nagashima, who was later to work with Maki in Tokyo.

Public space

Maki's initial spatial studies, be they for urban projects or individual buildings, were prima-

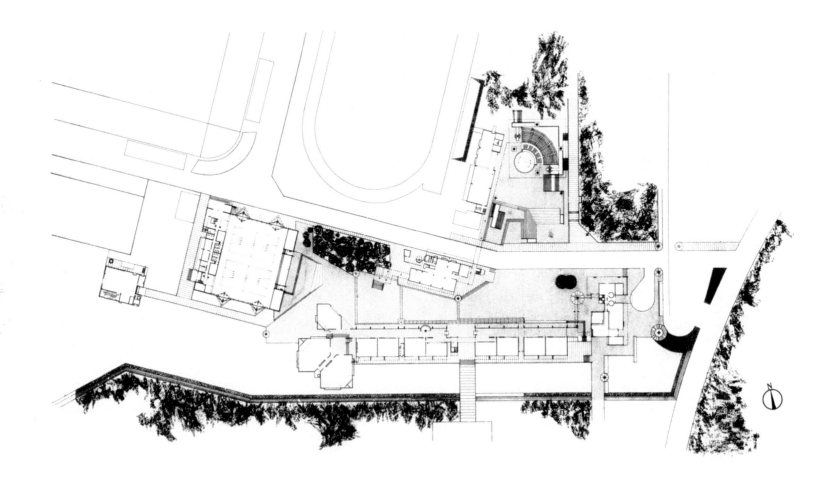

Rissho University, Kumagaya Campus, 1967–68.
Site plan.

rily concerned with public space and, consequently, directly or indirectly with urban space. The very notion of public space, in the Western sense, is foreign to the Japanese culture, wherein a defined urban space is clearly demarcated and accorded a certain level of privacy. That which is "between" or "without" carries spatial connotations alien to the Western idea of a public zone. Today Japanese "outside" space still retains a particular nature incompatible with Western notions of "planning" and "design". Consequently Maki's experience with Western planning through Tange's studio, and his extensive urban studies in the United States, placed him in a unique position with regard to urban design in Japan in the 1960s. The title he gave the firm he founded in Tokyo in 1965, Maki Associates, Design, Planning and Development, in itself established his particular expertise and set him apart from mainstream architectural practice in the country. His "public" space tends to be a defined space in keeping with the semi-public or semi-private nature of Japanese spatial definitions. These spaces fall into two main types: first, the open space or "plaza", in kinship with, say, the medieval temple compound, the first major spaces in Japan that the populace were allowed to enter; and second, the enclosed space, described in some of Maki's writings and planning projects as the "city room". Maki's plaza type is described by Hiroyuki Suzuki as "a kind of negative structure resulting from the act of not erecting something on a given piece of land".[22] The "city room" was first conceived as a new focal point of communication – more in the nature of the twentieth-century spaces of Tokyo's great railway stations, such as Shinjuku. The city room developed out of Maki's theory that in city growth, as density increases, what was exterior space becomes enveloped, resulting

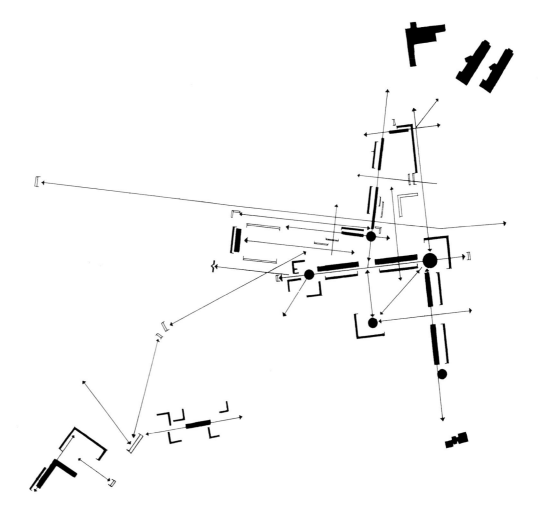

in interior exterior space. This particular morphological thinking of form consuming space was instrumental in suggesting ways towards creating interior public social space. These fundamental morphological and functional directives gave rise to the basic structuring of all his building and urban projects of the 1960s and early 1970s.

Plazas

Writing in 1992, Maki pointed to the absence of European-type plazas, *hiroba* (literally "wide open spaces") in Japanese cities, but the presence of countless plazas of the Japanese kind.[23] He proposed the equivalent of the *niwa,* a semi-public open space where ceremonies and events were traditionally performed (such as the walled compound of a temple), and the *meisho,* a more public space, which was initially a scenic place for reading poetry and later a spot where the populace gathered for festivals. Maki's "plazas" are neither *hiroba* or *niwa* but, as with so many features of his architecture, they exhibit a combination or blending of both. Certainly at Rissho University, the major and subsidiary open spaces might better be referred to as "courtyards", suggesting a type of enclosure and usage closer to the *niwa* rather than one conjured up by Maki's choice of the word "plaza".

Rissho University

In 1966 Maki commenced a two-stage design for the new Kumagaya Campus at Rissho University. This major planning and architectural project gave him the opportunity to implement his theories of spatial organisation for a vital and participatory "urban" prototype. In accord with the premises of "group form", the campus was organised as two clusters of buildings loosely related, in this case along two primary axes set at 30 degrees to each other, and a

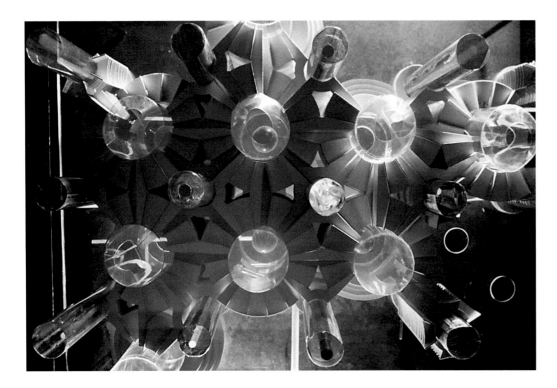

Golgi Structures, 1965.

defining major exterior space with several ancillary spaces.[24] The order of the composition is not clearly evident, causing Masataka Ogawa to comment, "An aerial view of the present campus reveals buildings facing a long, beltlike open space in an arrangement of subtle disorder."[25] The most evident element stabilising the composition is a long rectangular block that edges the "plaza" and acts as a static and fixed unit against which the remaining free-form buildings are arranged. The Mogusa Town Center design of 1969 employs a similar strategy. There, Maki established a dynamic and varied open space between the regular geometric blocks of the stores that define an L-shaped enclosure, giving anchorage to the loosely linked individual buildings of the bank and post office.

At Rissho University there is a high level of complexity and variety among the spatial units, and yet there is a remarkable cohesion, partly due to the uniform treatment of materials and details throughout. Despite little evidence of explicit control, the design was rationally planned in an exacting, analytical manner using projected geometries. The result is a remarkable cohesion in the grouping resulting from the establishment of a most careful series of visual relationships between buildings, in such a way that they appear to physically acknowledge one another and engage in dialogue across the intervening space.[26]

Rissho University Campus was rationalised on the basis that "the spatial system required to meet the demands of future society will thus be a dual system: one highly functional; the other extremely flexible."[27] Hence the functional spaces are particular to the nature of the activity to be performed, and the com-

ITE, Singapore, 2002. Sectional perspective.

munication spaces are the flexible spaces accommodating spontaneous and varied activities. The fundamental categories of space at Rissho are the "functional" special-use rooms such as the classrooms, libraries and gymnasiums, and the connecting "communication spaces" where all else takes place. The communication spaces dominate the planning, and in turn are subdivided into lineal "corridor" and "mall" spaces, static "station" spaces and expanses of space "plazas" serving both for rest and passage. These various types of spatial forms occur both inside and outside the buildings, merging through glazed walls and open arcades. There is a further hierarchical ordering within the subdivisions in areas such as the main plaza, itself distorted into a quasi-rectangular and a quasi-triangular zone. This centralising space contains extensive uninterrupted areas, smaller pockets

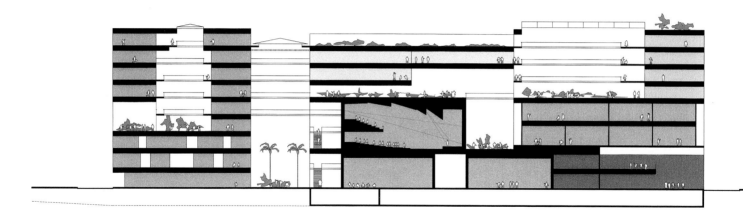

ITE, Singapore, 2002. Section.

of space, raised platforms at entry points (described by Maki as "stages" and intended to act as such for human encounters), and other differing zones inviting activities of various kinds. In 1971, in *Japan Architect,* Maki wrote poetically of the spaces and connections he was attempting to generate: "It seems that creating a place for human encounters involves expanding the territory of the building; that is, opening it as one might open a hand ... one can consider the plaza as this kind of open hand expanding the territory of a given building ... and ... I am fond of thinking about buildings that seem to be extending open hands towards each other in an overlapping of encounters."[28] Spatially the Rissho campus establishes an orchestration of diverse user-directed areas, convincingly demonstrating the planning concepts of Maki's theories of composition that here have established a dynamic balance, uniting objects and forming space without the stasis of conventionally ordered compositional design.

Golgi structures/City rooms

In the early 1960s, in parallel with his planning projects for city development, Maki had undertaken complementary abstract studies of urban growth. These took the form of three-dimensional exercises concerning the encapsulation of exterior public space along biological principles. Maki entitled them "Golgi structures", after the Golgi body discovered by the neurologist Camillo Golgi. These Golgi bodies involved multi-polar cells capable of relating to other cells in the system.[29] From this Maki developed a theory of possible connections, established between various centers in a city. Working with very abstract models, Maki commenced forming the city by designing its voids, that is, its streets and squares, then followed with the buildings, which increased in density over time. That is, the exterior spaces gave form to the solids. The original outdoor spaces became engulfed and became interior spaces which, because of their origins as outdoor spaces, retained their public nature and function. In 1967 Maki wrote, "The point to be made is that as volumetric density (of a building or building complex) increases, the influence of the external space on the final form of the building becomes very great ... interior development tends to become a consequence of the preset exterior space, and in the process converts this preset exterior space into a kind of interiorized exterior space."[30] Later, he expressed a similar reciprocal connection in his sketchbook, where he wrote, "Exterior spaces penetrate the inside, just as exterior spaces extend outside. The boundary of a building is where the two different kinds of spaces quarrel."[31] Maki's ITE Proposal for Singapore, 2002, shows his continuing interest in this form of thinking about the city, which had attained its most extensive expression in the permeable volumes of the Hillside Terraces that followed the long tradition of celebrating "in-between" spaces.

Although the Kumagaya Campus of Rissho University was primarily an exercise in spatial design in urban terms, its principal entry-gathering space, an heroic multi-level room containing a monumental staircase (the first of Maki's memorable interior stairs), can be read as an example of Maki's notion of a "city room", or as representative of his understanding of interior "outdoor" space. The "city room", an undefined multi-functional node located at a strategic position in the city, provided the focal point within a multi-level hier-

Civic Center, Senri New Town, Yokohama, 1969.

Civic Center, Senri New Town, Yokohama, 1969. Mezzanine plan.

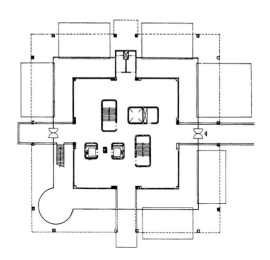

archy of connections referred to as "city corridors". Maki writes, "Linkage is simply the glue of the city. It is the act by which we unite all the layers of activity and resulting form in the city ... Ultimately, linkage is assembling patterns of experience in cities."[32] The concept of city rooms and linkages derives from the "city room" studies that he explored in *Movement Systems in the City*. Seminal also was the 1961, and modified 1963, proposal for the mixed development for the Dojima area of Osaka – that contained shared communal services and two "city room" plazas seen as "oases".[33] This large project was organised around movement systems with connections for future development. Commenting on Maki's work in his 1963 *An Architectural Journey in Japan*, J. M. Richards wrote, "In 1961 he published (in conjunction with Takenaka contracting company)

an unusually far-sighted redevelopment plan for the Dojima area of Osaka, just across the river from the main business center, in which he introduced the idea of the pedestrian precinct and the super-block containing communal services."[34] In *Movement Systems in the City*, Maki describes the "city room" as a place of movement, of systems interchange and information exchange. But most importantly, its functions would make it a gathering place where "human activities converge, interact, and are re-diverted". Further, it would be a "transitional place in terms of human experience – from oneself to fellow citizens".[35] The Boston plan was based on a system consisting of nodal points laced together by movement corridors of various kinds, in a manner reminiscent of the urban structure of Tokyo, where the order is provided by the rail networks and

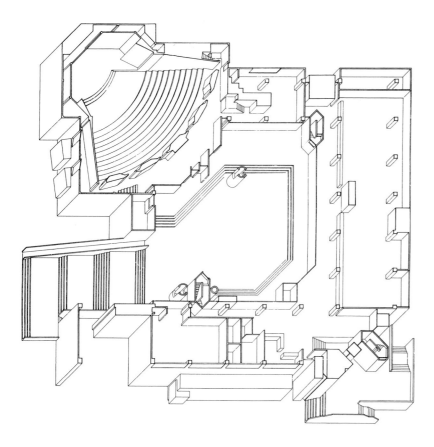

their stations. In the Boston study the nodal points were to be vast interior gathering-places for the social life of the city: sheltered, truly public spaces for the coming-together of people and activities. The "city room" actually or notionally appears in most of Maki's early projects, as at Rissho, the Civic Center at Senri New Town, 1969, the Kanazawa Ward Office and Community Center, Yokohama, 1974, and the Tsukuba University Central Building for Physical Education and Art, 1974.

In the Golgi structures the starting point was an abstract conception of public space shaped to receive activities, and in the "city room" the starting point was gathering and exchange requiring definition and shelter – the two complementary in their balancing of the positions of the action and space. The Golgi structure explorations and the "city room" studies opened up lines of thought which are given form in Maki's first significant urban gestures.

Senri New Town

At Senri, Maki's concern was to apply his thinking on spatial constructs to the inside and outside spaces and public and private relationships of a single, politically significant building in a public square. The project provided an excellent testing ground, as it connected exterior and interior public space in a multi-use facility with office space for private and face-to-face city business, cultural and educational theaters and meeting rooms, social activity spaces such as wedding halls, and commercial facilities with banks and shops. As with most of Maki's buildings of this time, the Senri Civic Center is set apart from its surroundings by a clearly demarcated open zone, in this case an elevated podium (which translates into Japanese as "raised *za*") containing terraces on various levels. The explicit definition of edges in these buildings recalls the enclosure of the *niwa*.

The building is unquestionably a "city room" whose planning rationales based on an internal zone mediating between the exterior plazas and the inner core facilities. This zone is multi-functional in the facilities it contains, but is also a generous circulation "communicating" area, intended to operate in the same way as the plaza and gathering lobby at Rissho University. The space was envisaged as an exhibition area, with the display panels, designed by Maki and Associates, contributing to the vitality of the scene. Communication routes cross this space at differing levels, re-

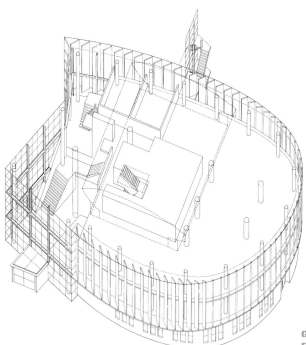

Graduate Research Center, Keio University,
Fujisawa Campus. 1994. Axonometric.

vealing the activities of the building and seeking to arouse interest and participation in the various offerings it contains for the people of Senri. Maki had high expectations of the project and was disappointed with the results of the application of his ideas and the lack of interest shown by the administrative staff in providing the happenings anticipated.[36] Nevertheless, Senri Civic Center represented an original and concerted effort to provide an inviting and open public building, with an interior space that was public in the same way as an open town square.

Kanazawa

The project for the Kanazawa Ward Offices commenced at the time that the Senri Civic Center was reaching completion. It extends the spatial explorations begun at Senri, but now, despite the restricted, contained site, it is designed as a more open composition, allowing scope to explore fresh spatial experiences. However, it would seem that at Kanazawa Maki

took a step back from the quite radical multi-level thinking evident in the spatial organisation of the Senri design. The design opens up the Ward Offices with a courtyard that is certainly in the spirit of the public "city room", but this time it is unroofed and overlooked by the surrounding areas through glass walls, rather than being internalised and consciously inter-meshed with the particular functional spaces as at Senri. It was intended, however, to operate as a Golgi structure designed to enhance individuals' awareness of others through the glass walls, and therefore enhance social relationships. The building, once again elevated on a podium, is intentionally defensive against its noisy site, and hides behind the solid walls of the rectangular building blocks lining two sides. As in previous projects, Maki counter-poises the rigid geometry of the site-defining blocks with the more freely formed objects of the composition, in this example that of the auditorium block. Due to its more restrained design, Kanazawa Ward Offices lacks the ten-

sion that is evident in the interior spaces of Senri Civic Center; it is more spatially relaxed and certainly more functionally resolved.

Tsukuba

The most successful of Maki's "city rooms" from this early stage of development is the vast roofed and partially enclosed central space of Tsukuba University Central Building. As with Maki's 1961 Toyoda Hall at Nagoya University, which stands at the end of a new highway and forms a visual gate to the main axis of the University, the building at Tsukuba bridges the principal axis of the campus forming a vast gateway. This severe but hand-some glass-block building is one of Maki's few projects – another being the Toyoda Hall – that gain their strength and formality, in part, from a certain level of symmetry. The central public space not only separates and links two areas of the campus but also serves to mediate between the different faculties housed in the wings to either side. Once more, the central

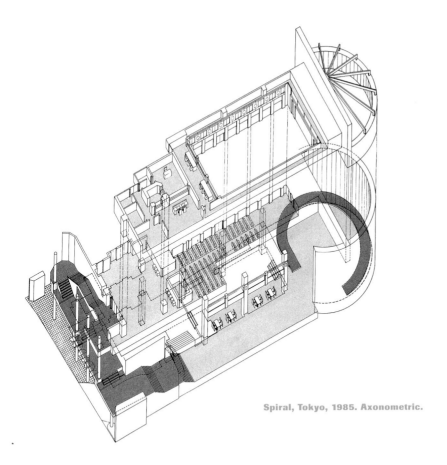

Spiral, Tokyo, 1985. Axonometric.

Spiral, Tokyo, 1985.

"station" is a most heroic space rising the full height of the building and again containing an arresting stair. In this case, a dramatic, sculptural, open, geometrical steel staircase links the five upper levels. This central gateway space or "well" of Tsukuba University, that is both indoors and outdoors, is charged with movement generated within the building and from across the campus. At the same time, it provides for the parking as well as riding of bicycles, the chatting of groups, and the drinking of coffee.

Maki's plazas and "city rooms" have no direct precedent in the traditional organisation or even spatial thinking of Japanese town planning. At the same time, the underlying pattern of thought, which is activity, then enclosure, then the filling of the emptiness, and so on, is essentially Japanese. Marlin

expressed the very essence of the nature of Maki's spaces when he wrote of Tsukuba University "... this emptiness that he made room for, here – that vacuum which, it turns out, cannot help but be full – of color and light and motion – because it was *meant* to be a receptive receptacle ... ."[37]

The approach and themes established in these early projects are discernible in Maki's future work. The "plaza" or the "city room" appears in one form or another in most of his urban designs. The "loft" research space that dominates the design of the Graduate Research Center at Keio University Fujisawa Campus, 1993, may be seen as a sequel to the city room idea, celebrating not only the gathering of the research workers but the coming together of

people in study groups from all over the world via electronic transmission.[38] Spiral, 1985, presents a highly developed city room offering a new kind of space where people can congregate surrounded by cultural and commercial activities. Maki states, "The significance of the building lies in the new social space."[39]

More recently, the MIT Media Laboratories, organised as a three-dimensional matrix of interlocking spaces, follow the "city room" notion. The two-tiered central atrium contains public areas, and serves as the connecting link to the existing media laboratory. Double-height laboratory units surround this atrium to create a continuous cascade of interrelated space. This building, scheduled for completion in 2005, carries the theme from the 1960s into the new century.

Notes

1 In "An outside view of the enigma of Japanese architecture", *The Japan Architect,* 52, 3, March 1977, pp. 72–84, I attempted to express this condition. For an excellent discussion of the Japanese city see Barrie Shelton, *Learning from the Japanese City: West Meets East in Urban Design,* London, E & FN Spon, 1999.

2 With the obvious exception of Sapporo.

3 Yasufumi Kijima, "A portrait of the architect as a young Japanese", *Domus* (618), July 1981, p. 34.

4 Noël Burch, *To the Distant Observer: Form and Meaning in Japanese Cinema,* London, Scholar Press, 1979, p. 281.

5 Botond Bognar, *Contemporary Japanese Architecture: Its Development and Challenge,* New York, Van Nostrand Reinhold, 1985, p. 84, reports that 4,200,000 homes were destroyed, which was one quarter of all the homes. 119 cities were damaged; in 28 more than 70 percent of homes were destroyed and in 10 more than 80–90 percent were destroyed.

6 Isozaki worked with Tange on *A Plan for Tokyo,* 1960. Tange showed "Sea City" and "Tower City" by Kikutake at the Otterloo meeting of CIAM.

7 As early as 1958 proposals had been made for filling in parts of Tokyo Bay.

8 Refer to the joint publication K. Kikutake, N. Kawazoe, M. Ohtaka, F. Maki and N. Kurokawa, *Metabolism: The Proposals for New Urbanism,* Tokyo, Bijutsu Shuppansha, 1960.

9 Fumihiko Maki, "The theory of group form", *The Japan Architect,* 45, 2 (161), February 1970, p. 39.

10 Noboru Kawazoe, "Introduction", *Metabolism: The Proposals for New Urbanism.*

11 Dojima Project and K Project with Takenaka Co.

12 Kiyonori Kikutake, "Ocean City", *Metabolism: The Proposals for New Urbanism,* p. 13.

13 Kisho Kurokawa, "Space City", *Metabolism: The Proposals for New Urbanism,* p. 80. Nakagin Capsule Tower, Tokyo, 1972, and his "Beautilion" Tower at Expo '70, Osaka, provided opportunities for the application of ordering principles based on fixed and plug-in parts.

14 Erhard Hursch, *Tokyo,* Tokyo, Charles E. Tuttle, 1965 (no pagination).

15 Chris Fawcett, *The New Japanese House: Ritual and Anti-ritual: Patterns of Dwelling,* New York, Harper Row, 1980, p. 17.

16 Fawcett, *The New Japanese House: Ritual and Anti-ritual: Patterns of Dwelling,* p. 17.

17 A part of Kikutake's floating city was eventually built as Aquapolis for the Okinawa Expo '75.

18 Paul and Percival Goodman, *Communitas,* Tokyo, Shokokusha, 1967 (translated by Fumihiko Maki).

19 Bernard Rudofsky, *Architecture Without Architects: A Short Introduction to Nonpedigreed Architecture,* New York, Museum of Modern Art, 1964.

20 Fumihiko Maki, *Movement Systems in the City,* Cambridge, Mass., Graduate School of Design, Harvard University, 1965.

21 Fumihiko Maki and Kawazoe Noboru, *What is Urban Space?,* Tokyo, Tsukuba Publishing, 1970.

22 Hiroyuki Suzuki, "Context and manner in the works of Fumihiko Maki", *The Japan Architect,* 54, 5 (265), May 1979, p. 67.

23 Fumihiko Maki, "Hiroba and Niwa (unpublished English translation)", trans. Hiroshi Watanabe, *Kioku No Keisyo: A Collection of Essays,* Tokyo, Kajima Publishing Co., 1992.

24 The final stage of the project was not built.

25 Masataka Ogawa, "Fumihiko Maki – Frontiers of contemporary Japanese art", *The Japan Architect,* 48, 3 (195), March 1973, p. 82.

26 How this is actually achieved in terms of physical planning is well explained in "Campus of many spaces", *The Architectural Forum,* May 1970, pp. 35–39.

27 "The Rissho campus and public spaces", unpublished Maki and Associates document, 1968, p. 6.

28 Fumihiko Maki, "Thoughts about plazas; recollections. From the Nagoya University Toyoda Memorial Hall to the Consolidated Offices of Kanazawa Ward, Yokohama", *The Japan Architect,* 46, 12 (180), December 1971, pp. 39–50. The metaphor of the open hand was also used by Aldo van Eyck, and in a quite different way by Le Corbusier at Chandigarh.

29 Ross writes, "The Golgi body was named for Camillo Golgi, a nineteenth-century Italian physiologist noted for his basic research in neurology. In 1883 his studies of the central nervous system revealed multi-polar cells which had the ability to establish connections with other nerve cells. This research eventually led another scientist to discover the neuron." Michael Franklin Ross, *Beyond Metabolism: The New Japanese Architecture,* New York, Architectural Record: A McGraw-Hill Publication, 1978, p. 30. See Ross for photo and description, p. 32.

30 Fumihiko Maki, "Four studies in collective form – A summary", unpublished Maki and Associates document, August 1967, p. 1.

31 Fumihiko Maki, *Fragmentary Figures: The Collected Architectural Drawings,* Tokyo, Kyuryudo Art Publishing, 1989 (no pagination).

32 Fumihiko Maki, from "Notes on collective form", as published in *The Japan Architect,* 16, Special Issue on Fumihiko Maki, Winter 1994, p. 269.

33 Fumihiko Maki, "Skyscrapers at last", (No. 4 in the series "The Re-making of Japan", pp. 139–43 unidentified source).

34 J. M. Richards, *An Architectural Journey in Japan,* London, The Architectural Press, 1963, p. 185. Maki was fortunate in having family connections with one of Japan's largest building corporations, Takenaka Corporation, which assisted in the establishment of his practice by making work available to him.

35 Maki, *Movement Systems in the City,* p. 17.

36 Maki, "Thoughts about plazas", p. 42.

37 William Marlin, "The growing of grids: Central Building Tsukuba University", *Architectural Record,* April 1977, p. 111.

38 Fumihiko Maki, "Space, image and materiality", *The Japan Architect,* 16, Special Issue on Fumihiko Maki, Winter 1994, p. 8.

39 Conversation with Maki, Tokyo, 1995.

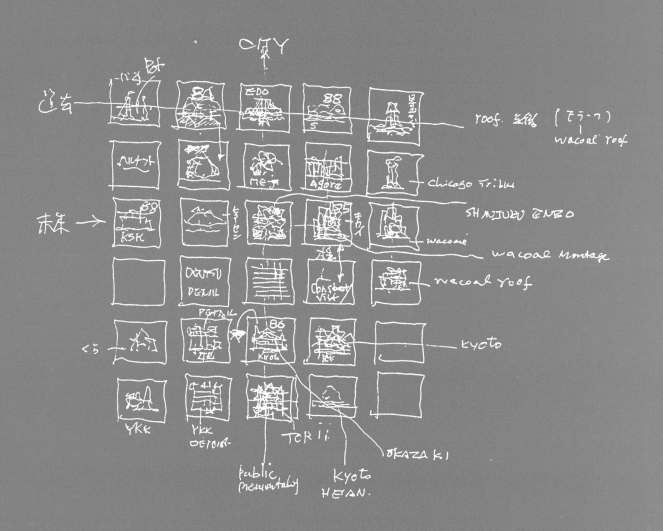

Impression note

4 Order: The Choreography of Order

Of all the fundamental principles discoverable in Japanese architecture the most sweeping and at the same time the most profound is a pervasive sense of order – a precise organization of the architecture that extends almost effortlessly to a breadth and depth of control, welding together the inherent patterns of form and space into a unique organic whole.[1]

Carver goes on to say that "a long history of primitive contact with nature developed in the Japanese a profound respect for natural form: in it they found evidence of a larger order to which they felt inexorably linked."[2] From his very first projects Maki has seen the role of the designer as "charged with giving form – with perceiving and contributing order".[3] Maki's designs, be they of urban or detail scale, are balanced within a conceptual net of instinctive, guiding and controlling directives. These directives then become tools of working and of shaping the solution while remaining elusive rather than evident.

Throughout history, the built environment had been structured – consciously or unconsciously – to reflect the spiritual and social order of the culture that produced it. The city and its buildings, their status, placement and organization were comprehended in terms of a given cultural framework. The pattern of the city revealed its nature; groups of buildings established relationships and defined space; individual buildings, according to their dimension and demeanour, told of their standing and value. The total environment offered messages that the individual could read and understand. The highways and skyscrapers of the modern city continued to provide a comprehensible and revealing order. It is generally accepted that the context for life in the twenty-first century will become increasingly expansive and homogenous, and embrace both physical and virtual worlds. Contemporary architectural and social theories share a common concern as to the capability of the future city and its buildings to continue to attain such readable patterns of relationships between the unit and the totality, the specific and the general, and the individual and the global community. Critical is the identification of a means of providing environments that accommodate the universal condition but also allow for personal identity, orientation and direction.

One might well ask "What is order?" In this context one could echo Aldo van Eyck in saying "order is that which makes chaos possible", adding, "that which makes knowledge possible".[4] Notions of order have been radically revised with the acceptance of complexity and chaos in expanding theories of physics. Notwithstanding this, Japanese comprehensions of order have never been marked by the clarity and rigidity that characterised the Aristotelian and Cartesian disciplines of Western thought. As Carver explains, "All relationships are abbreviated and subtle, encouraging the exercise of the imagination in grasping the whole." Like many expressions in Japan, order is not necessarily evident, but hidden.[5]

Maki's work of the 1960s established the principles that have served throughout his career as a framework to provide a dynamic "order" that accommodates the fluctuations of time. Maki's "order" is derived from his understanding of the relationship of part to whole, giving rise to determining precepts across a spectrum ranging from the building's place in the context of history, to the individual in the context of the city. The designs embody orders and patterns of organisation that give them coherence without rigidity. The ordering means vary through time in response to the changing context. Further, for a comprehension of Maki's work it is necessary to extend the understanding of context to all scales. That is, the part is related to the whole in the same unfixed and reciprocal manner, whether it is building to city or element to building or detail to element. In his early travels Maki had identified such relationships in the aesthetic of vernacular towns where individual elements retain their vitality despite their blending into the totality of the composition. Yet for Maki the notion of part to whole embraces social as well as physical associations. The building is seen as the artefact embodying and transmitting the order of time and place and thus providing orientation and identity.

Part to whole

In the essay "Toward group form", Maki and Ohtaka wrote, "For, although we are conscious of the architectural development of the indi-

vidual buildings that are elements of the group, we try also to create a total image through the group, that is again a reflection of growth and decay in our life process. This is an effort to conceive a form in relationship to an ever-changing whole and its parts."[6] "Toward group form", set forth the distinction between Alberti's static dictum of beauty and the closed composition, and the dynamic composition proposed by "group form". It stated that Alberti's static "relationship between the elements and the totality may be represented as TOTALITY $= \sum$ ELEMENTS and the balance thus obtained is destroyed at the moment a single element is taken out of the group. In the group form, on the other hand, the relationship is represented as TOTALITY $\supset \sum$ ELEMENTS, where $\supset$ = inclusion. Here totality embraces the elements; in other words, the total image of the group is not basically altered, even though some elements are taken out, or different elements added."[7]

Yet Maki warns, "For each part to be meaningful in relation to the whole, for the whole to regulate its component parts, and for tension to exist between the two, can be called ideal conditions for architecture. But these conditions are easier described than achieved. If the whole is determined too simplistically, the parts loose individual identity. If the parts are

too individuated, the whole fails to achieve organic unity."[8]

Context

A dialogue between the various components of a program produces an architecture both distinct and particular to place. In Maki's case this led to the term "contextual" being applied to his work by various critics in the 1980s.[9] In light of later uses of the term in architecture, its application can be misleading when used in reference to Maki's architecture, which rarely derives directly from the particular visual characteristics of place. For although Maki has said that "a sensitive response to place is required by every architect",[10] he has further claimed that the architect must meet questions of deciding how to react to the environment or determining new qualities with which to invest it. Maki's buildings, hence, operate with the given circumstance more in a transforming manner. For, as Hiroshi Watanabe points out, "in Japan there isn't much of a context in the Western sense."[11] Japanese respond to place by changing it, or adding to it, rather than by being changed by it or taking from it. Clearly demonstrative of such encounters is the theater of the Floating Pavilion for Groningen in Holland, 1996, which transforms each site it visits in terms of form and program.

Floating Pavilion, Groningen, Holland, 1996.

Maki's particular form of contextualism was explored in both his early urban plans and his model studies of the Golgi structures. Basically it involves relationships within systems which arise and develop from the initial juxtapositions and the changes that occur with time. That is, in a collective, forms "grow in a system ... The element and growth pattern are reciprocal – both in design and operation ... a kind of a feedback process."[12] The framework for Maki's "contextualism" is established by the notion of the pattern of metabolic change, and the vital exchanges inherent in his theories of the reciprocal, evolving nature of individual/collective partnerships.

Maki's architecture also may respond to place by rejecting it entirely, turning from it and providing the building's own ambience. So although the architecture is strongly determined by context, the relationship may not necessarily be one of accord and is certainly not subservient. The Japanese historical means of site planning, *za*, might clarify certain attitudes inherent in Maki's approach to place-making. Maki has discussed *za* as a seat, a place for a thing or an activity. He writes, "*Za* was a concept created to relate, in actual fact or on a symbolic plane, diverse heterogenous elements existing within and without a certain domain. Various independ-

Prefectural Sports Center, Osaka, 1972.

St Mary's International School. Tokyo, 1972.

ent elements are, for example, connected, supported or subordinated by *za.*" And further, "*Za* can also be said to be a means of actualising the latent energy of a site that is at first glance impoverished and unattractive."[13]

Certain fundamental propositions underlie Maki's studies in, and designs of, social space. The first and second are reciprocal and complementary and give rise to the hermeneutical third proposition. The first is that architectural space exists for human events and is generated by them. The second is that space is the generator or fountainhead of human activity, thus establishing the third proposition that design and development arise from never-ending chains of exchanges and feedbacks between spaces and activities.

The term "contextual" is valid for Maki if used in the sense that architecture can only be understood or become meaningful when seen in the context of both circumstance and culture, as it is responsive to both time and place. Maki's contextualism is well summed up by his 1970 comment: "The ultimate aim of architecture is to create spaces to serve mankind, and in order to achieve this, the architect must understand human activities from the standpoints of history, ecology, and action circumstances."[14] This perspective on the intention of architecture, and the global view necessary to achieve it, remains exceptional among the Japanese avant-garde. Maki writes, however, of his interest in buildings suitable for their given physical contexts. He differentiates, for example, between his response to the pleasant

tree-lined street of the site of St Mary's International School, where the building is divided into small parts and threaded into the existing environmental whole, and his response to the Osaka Prefectural Sports Center, where the spatial unit is contained as a single entity as it was felt that a powerful form was necessary for that particular site. At the Sports Center the roof slopes down towards the nearby housing, but rises and thrusts forward on the canal side to be in scale with the nearby factories. Writing in *Contemporary Architects* of Maki's "enormous" structures Ching-Yu Chang comments, "It is apparent that the thrust of his design attention is not the glorification of these concepts, but the successful deployment of them to create inclusive highly contextual architecture that is in strict accord with

human, psychological preferences."[15] This ability to deal with advanced, large-size, technological structures in a relative and humane way continues to distinguish Maki's designs for the large structures of the 1990s.

The writings and projects of Maki's early career testify to his initial concerns with responding to the given situation and establishing a shared rapport between the architectural solution and the site, program, cultural background, behavioural patterns, community needs, urban conditions and global circumstances. This rapport is sought in both physical and social terms, and has been referred to by Maki as "ecological equilibrium" and "social equilibrium".[16] What is meant by this was spelt out in 1968 with regard to the genesis of the design of Rissho University: "Any evaluation of them (architectural spaces) must take into account not only the physical environment but the total 'situation' resulting from the interaction between human activity and physical environment."[17] Here the interaction of a micro-scale system of parts with a macro-scale system of materials and site-planning produces a remarkably convincing solution in line with Maki's intention.

Conversation

Writing in the 1980s, in *The Practice of Everyday Life*, de Certeau determined the need for a shift in the role of the city designer from one involved solely with the composition of urban form in a material and spatial sense, to one concerned with design in the temporal dimension: that is, the inclusion of a design dimension that occupies space but is unbounded by it in any restrictive sense; one concerned with possibilities and with action. He uses the terms "strategist" and "tactician" to define these roles, seeing today's conventional urban designer cast in the spatially grounded "strategist" role, involved with the fixing of boundary and the definition of space. On the other hand, he considers the "tactician" as the one who views the situation in terms of the human event. In order to accommodate the "tactician", the "strategist" must resist "design" and provide an "undesigned", unfixed, permeable and adaptive setting with the potential for involvement and action.[18]

Maki's writings and works of the 1960s clearly evidence his dual role first as a "tactician" and then as a "strategist". As William Marlin suggests, with the design for Tsukuba University Central Building Maki might well have asked himself, "Which is more important, the nature of walking or the walkway itself?" Marlin gives the reply, "The walking was, of course."[19] Further, even in such early works, Maki adopted a hermeneutical approach to design, seeing the design roles of "tactician" and "strategist" as complementary with a constant reciprocal exchange between the two. He extended this notion of exchange to embrace the relationship between design and the situation, describing it as the architect's "conversation" with what is in time and space.

Such thinking reflects both traditional Japanese notions of the relationship between space, time and design, and Western post-structuralist theory, revealing an affinity between the two. In its constructs and connections Maki's architecture portrays a shifting understanding of the world order of the time and the individual's relationship to it. This is reflected in the associations established in his work as it sustains the hermeneutical exchange within collectives in his early studies on "group form", exemplified in the design of Rissho University Campus, to the classicism of his work of the 1970s, and to his theories of fracturing and incomplete wholes illustrated in the facade of the Wacoal Building, also known as Spiral, of the 1980s. Interestingly, the major design projects of the late 1980s and 1990s, such as the campus for Keio University, Fujisawa, reveal a rationalistic order in contrast to the loose dynamic interplay that characterises the smaller individual projects of that time.

Maki's position arises from concern regarding the architect's responsibility for the good or bad effects of the intervention. What he considers as appropriate is derived from certain understandings of relationships between objects, and between people and objects, filtered through the private world of the architect. Basically it is an interpretive reading with a shared exchange between the participants. In all cases the relationship and the responses will arise from the given conditions. He uses the term "rapport" to describe the relationship he seeks between the program, the environment and the building – this

is a matter of taking from and giving to the rich resources of the place. This is the intention of the architect's conversation, which, in Maki's view, comes from a dialogue between the particular situation, the technical resources available, and the cultural resources of history which include much of the world's inherited knowledge, traditions, racial culture and philosophies. The conversation is between what the architect contributes to the exchange and what is provided. The architect's contribution has been described by Maki as coming from his "primary landscape" or "imaginary landscape" – that which is personal to the individual. Maki draws on the book *The Primary Landscapes of Literature (Bungaku ni okeru genfukei)*, by Takeo Okuno, to help explain what he sees as the private contribution that the architect brings to design.[20] As described by Okuno, the primary landscape of the individual is not just the outcome of past experiences and impressions but is inherited through culture and family as well. Maki also uses the term "inner landscape", referring to the personal landscape of each individual, which is what the architect brings to each project.

Given this holistic view, it is interesting that, for Maki the urbanist, nature and the natural landscape have not been strongly influential in fashioning his work in a material or metaphorical sense. On a philosophical level, nature seems not to loom large in Maki's imagination. He tends not to write about it, or talk about it, or to use it as an analogy for his

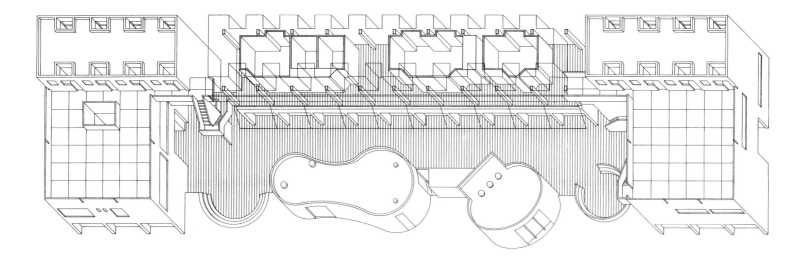

Mogusa Town Center, Tokyo, 1969. Isometric.

architecture. It is, however, of note that the inspiration for the Metabolist movement was organic in nature. On the other hand, Maki's buildings of the 1960s are often explicitly defined as man-made, intellectually conceived works, independent of the world of nature. Whereas nature figures strongly in much Japanese contemporary design (in a spiritual and tangible sense with Tadao Ando, as a transitional medium for the generation of form by Itsuko Hasegawa, or as an analogy for Arata Isozaki), Maki's architecture, until the 1990s, remains surprisingly distant from considerations or contemplations of "nature" as a concept for inspiration or as a material for manipulation. As Kengo Kuma points out, "For those people nature is a kind of philosophy, but Maki's view is more traditional. For Maki the Center is always man. Human beings are the Center. Nature is outside. The experience of human beings is the first thing for him with the architecture secondary. This is the concern of Japanese traditional buildings."[21] As

well as a conceptual remoteness from nature, in Maki's early buildings planting did not figure as a major compositional material. The first major exception, the Toyota Guest House, 1974, swings to the other pole, with an organic blending of building and landscape, both in its setting and the interior spaces.

Orientation – identity

All this leads to the ultimate intention of the ordering of the environment, which is to offer a satisfying, livable context for existence, providing a sense of where one is and who one is. Maki's "ecological equilibrium" and "social equilibrium" are descriptive of, in the first case, an attuned yet balanced setting, providing an orientating and a meaningful dialogue, and, in the second, a comfortable and comprehensible ambience, satisfying in both its familiarity and its challenge. In both cases, the primary context is seen as that of the city, with the responsibility for its realisation vested in the urban designer.

Such a concern for the need for territorial awareness and a sense of belonging was not common in Japanese urban theory of the 1960s. Maki had been exposed in the United States to the work of Jane Jacobs, Kevin Lynch, Christopher Alexander and others, and the social and psychological basis of his work must, in part, be indebted to the new movement of social and community concern being voiced in America at the time of his university appointments in that country.[22] Certainly he was influenced by the humanistic spokesmen from Team X, notably the teachings of van Eyck. The transposition of such concerns to Japan in the 1960s constituted a significant contribution to urban social awareness.

Among his concerns at this time was the seen need to devise modes of ordering or giving pattern or recognition to an environment so that it provides orientation and indications of possible action. Such an order and comprehensibility is seen as emerging from the revelation of a human order hidden within the city,

and from the provision of significant monuments and meaningful landmarks. The audience is the user and the passer-by, both of whom derive identity and knowledge from the city plan, the solid and spatial urban morphology, and building form and detail. Maki writes of "attempting to give the users of a building a place directly related to their identities and at the same time trying to develop some kind of relationship with people who merely pass by the building". Hence, Maki calls for clear communication from streets, space and individual buildings through being both physically memorable and revealing of intention, purpose and connections. He further writes that, "a building should be able to reveal its purport, its role in the city, and its history at a single glance."[23]

The order of the city can reside in the apparently chaotic as well as in the evidently rational. The tasks of order are seen by Maki to be, first, one of providing either a sensed or discernible organisation and, second, one of revealing it. Further is the recognition of the need to stabilise volatile states in order to create. In the Boston study the word "chaos" was used not to refer to "the lack of structure, but to the difficulty of perceiving it: and the problem is not one of restructuring but of making understanding easier. A person moving through a city must be given visual clues and explanations of where he is and where he is going, of what these places are, and how they are related to each other."[24] Maki later wrote that at certain times we appreciate diversity but it can make us insensible; "then in our inability to order experience, we suffer the city, and long for some adequate means to comprehend it as a product of men like ourselves – as the product of an intelligent ordering force ... It [urban design] must recognise the meaning of the order it seeks to manufacture, a humanly significant, spatial order."[25] Spatial understanding is seen as psychologically uplifting and liberating, allowing for a more relaxed and intimate involvement with

Mogusa Town Center, Tokyo, 1969.

the city. Visual clarity is seen as necessary to help "the man who is in danger of losing his identity in a mammoth city".[26] Identity is interpreted as belonging most importantly to community with territory, recognised by an evident relationship between community and buildings. Maki calls for readable form from landmarks, such as church steeples or buildings high on sloping ground, to operate as physical markers identifying places particular to the individual, and, more importantly, to serve as symbols of shared values and local and urban group identity.

Choreography

The city is viewed by Maki as a stage where the designer provides not just the sets but the choreography for the performance. He writes, "For me, the architect is like a movie director

in that he attempts to develop a scenario by means of the design process and does not concentrate on static forms."[27] The stage is one to comfortably accommodate the daily patterns of living, and to provide for both community and individual spectacle (being seen). "We must not forget that double spectatorship – seeing and being seen, the thing seeing and the thing seen – is extremely important to the urban environment."[28] The major stair that flanks the glass street facade at Maki's Spiral Building in Tokyo provides for this dual exchange. Here chairs on the landings serve as observation posts for the movement on the street, while those passing by are allowed to look into the building. The scenario is acted out in the mind of the architect-director, who attempts to provide the scenery most supportive of the performance. Essential to the suc-

cess of the project is the architect's commitment to observation, and the translation of the results of this into a design of accommodation.

Maki's initial projects evidence a planning approach involving design to accommodate the user's expectations and likely psychological as well as practical needs. As examples he refers to the wishes and expectations of different social groups, citing the activities of the marketing housewife at the shopping center at Mogusa, a suburban zone of 2,400 households on the outskirts of Tokyo, and those of the window-shopper visiting the boutiques and galleries in fashionable Daikanyama. The user as an active and moving participant becomes the generator of the design. At Mogusa, for example, he saw the scenario as follows: "Commuters from the project take buses to reach the nearest train station. The bus stop is locat-

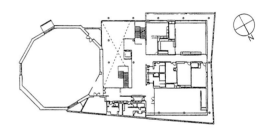

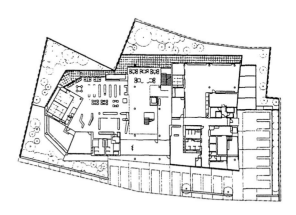

Shinohara Community Center. Yokohama, 1997. Plans.

ed in front of the Center. Shoppers are most active in the evening when housewives with their children come to wait for their husbands in the center. They enter through gates at both ends of the center then proceed to the shopping plaza. An overhang protects this long, narrow west-orientated plaza from the late afternoon sun. And on the second- and third-storey roofs children play hide-and-seek."[29] The comfort and convenience provided for through choreographic design is intended to impart a sense of involvement and an awareness of territory. The 1997 Shinohara Community Center, Yokohama, is one such place where the community has clearly taken over; there is a sense of possession and interaction as glass walls reveal the participants, such as the ballroom dancing class, to various users engaged in other pursuits.

Maki's seminal work of the 1960s was concerned with establishing a flexible order that would encourage, as well as accommodate, the growth and change of the physical and social structures of the city. Such an order would arise from hermeneutical relationships established between part and whole, participant and place, at all scales.

Such a concept of order is endemic in the inherited Japanese way of planning, as in *za*, and closely attuned to the postmodern reading of the shifting scenario of the electronic city. Order may be chaotic or rational but must be evident. In Maki's thinking, such communication would involve the plan, space and artefact. Most importantly for him, the order of the city must symbolise the collective, providing through its community and territory self-knowledge for the individual.

Maki's thinking on the choreography of order figures among his contributions to the evolution of the shifting theoretical positions that characterise both architecture and urban design. His proposals for generating space from activity, his temporal "cinematic" conception of design, his recognition of the hermeneutical basis of all design, his attempt to work with the dynamic and reality of the city in a reciprocal manner, and the social basis of the concerns, underlie this body of work.

Notes

1 Norman F. Carver, *Form and Space of Japanese Architecture,* Tokyo, Shokokusha, 1955, p. 8.

2 Carver, p. 16.

3 Fumihiko Maki, "Notes on collective form", reprinted in *The Japan Architect,* 16, Winter 1994, p. 254.

4 Conversation with Aldo van Eyck, Amsterdam, 1992.

5 Ashihara explores this condition in the city. Yoshinobu Ashihara, *Hidden Orders/ Tokyo Through the Twentieth Century,* Tokyo/New York, Kodansha International, 1989.

6 Fumihiko Maki and Masato Ohtaka, "Toward group form", *Metabolism: The Proposals for New Urbanism,* Tokyo, Bijutsu Shuppansha, 1960, p. 58.

7 Maki and Ohtaka, "Toward group form", p. 59.

8 Fumihiko Maki, "An environmental approach to architecture", *The Japan Architect,* 45, 3 (195), March 1973, p. 21.

9 For example Michael Franklin Ross, *Beyond Metabolism: The New Japanese Architecture,* New York, Architectural Record: A McGraw-Hill Publication, 1978 and Botond Bognar, *Contemporary Japanese Architecture: Its Development and Challenge,* New York, Van Nostrand Reinhold, 1985.

10 Fumihiko Maki, "Modernism at the crossroad", *The Japan Architect,* 35, 3 (311), March 1983, p. 22.

11 Conversation with Hiroshi Watanabe, Tokyo, 1995.

12 Maki, "Notes on collective form", p. 200.

13 Fumihiko Maki, "Stillness and plenitude – The architecture of Yoshio Taniguchi", *The Japan Architect,* 21, 1 (531), Spring 1996, p. 9.

14 Fumihiko Maki, "The theory of group form", *The Japan Architect,* 45, 2 (161), February 1970, p. 39.

15 Ching-Yu Chang, "Maki, Fumihiko", *Contemporary Architects,* 2nd edition, Chicago and London, St James Press, 1987, p. 506.

16 Fumihiko Maki, "The potential of planning", *Architecture in Australia,* 60, 4 (695), August 1971, p. 700.

17 "The Rissho campus and public spaces", unpublished Maki and Associates document, August 1968, p. 1.

18 Michel de Certeau, *The Practice of Everyday Life*, Berkeley, University of California Press, 1984.

19 William Marlin, "The growing of grids: Central Building Tsukuba University", *Architectural Record*, April 1977, pp. 107–12.

20 Maki, "An environmental approach to architecture", p. 20. Maki also discusses this book in Teijiro Muramatsu, "Humanity and architecture. Teijiro Muramatsu and leading Japanese architects. Dialogue Series 2: with Fumihiko Maki", *The Japan Architect*, 48, 9 (201), September 1973, p. 94.

21 Conversation with Kengo Kuma, Tokyo, 1995.

22 Maki met Jane Jacobs in 1956.

23 Fumihiko Maki, "Thoughts about plazas; recollections. From the Nagoya University Toyoda Memorial Hall to the Consolidated Offices of Kanazawa Ward, Yokohama", *The Japan Architect*, 46, 12 (180), December 1971, p. 39.

24 Fumihiko Maki, "Four studies in collective form – A summary", unpublished Maki and Associates document, August 1967, p. 3 (extract from *Movement Systems in the City*, Harvard University Graduate School of Design, Cambridge, Mass., 1965. p. 11.)

25 Maki, "Notes on collective form", p. 265.

26 Maki in Masataka Ogawa, "Fumihiko Maki – Frontiers of contemporary Japanese art", *The Japan Architect*, 48, 3 (195), March 1973, p. 83.

27 Maki, "An environmental approach to architecture", p. 20.

28 Maki, "The theory of group form", p. 41.

29 Maki, "The theory of group form", p. 19. Financial constraints prevented the erection of the awning.

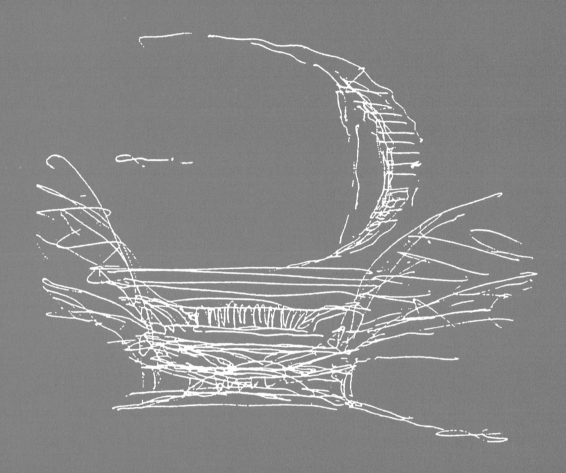

Fujisawa Gymnasium: Concept sketch.

5 Making: A Matter of Making

Technological possibility can be sanguinely useful only when it is a tool of civilised persons. Inhuman use of technological advance is all too frequently our course.[1]

The tempering of technology

The increasing dominance of technology in contemporary life carries enormous consequences for architecture and the city and demands a response. The consequences and potential of electronic technologies are more insidious and invasive than those of mechanical technologies. In Europe, the writings of Martin Heidegger hypothesised on the real nature of technology and our relationship to it. As Heidegger argued, both the rejection and the unqualified acceptance of technology carries dangers threatening to "Being-in-the-world".[2] Rather, he advocated an attitude of "letting-be" – an acceptance of technology's inevitability with a guarded and informed deployment of its services.

It can be argued that there is much accord between Heidegger's position and the attitude to life in general as embraced in traditional Japanese philosophy. Certainly, Kishio Kurokawa, in his extensive writings on the relationship of Japanese culture and Western influences, argues convincingly of the ability of the Japanese to modify and temper the harsher aspects of imported technologies.[3] To Maki, technology has always been a means to an end, never the *raison d'être* of the project. Clearly stating his position, Maki writes, "Moulding space is the most important act of architecture – it must be enclosed in a membrane. Where the membranes intersect or come together that is where the detail appears and technology enters in."[4] Technology contributes to the mindset that produces the image of space, and it is through technology that space is transformed into architecture. Technology, in part, generates the effects of program and context for architecture. Maki conceives of spaces to accommodate and counter those effects. He uses technology to enclose space, to modify enclosure, to enrich the enclosures, and to extend form.

As early as 1964 Maki wrote, "Homogenisation of the environment is not, as many people feel, the inevitable result of mass technology and communication. These same forces can produce entirely new products."[5] Later he argued that, although it may be true that systemised technology has given rise to homogeneity and neutrality in architecture, it is equally true the "technology can also make it possible for us to express diversity and complexity. Moreover, technology can have meaning in itself and increase the possible range of architectural expression."[6] Although technology increasingly creates physical and social problems, at the same time it provides the possibilities to alleviate these problems. That is, technology is the principal tool for fighting itself. Maki has always adopted a critical exploitative stance towards technology. He has been sensitive to the changes it has wrought and sensitive to its possibilities for performance and its ability to counter the effects of its own making. His work demonstrates creative design with tempered technology and exemplifies that accord can be found, and synthesis can be achieved, between the complementary and interwoven spirits of culture and technology. To him the technologies, physical and electronic, are means and not ends, yet they impinge strongly on both the creation and the imagery of his work. In the first case, they make possible the shaping of contemporary space; in the second case, they are realistically seen to represent where we are and what we are, and to embody the aspirations of the present and the future. "To me, technology is not universal at all. My definition of technology is the appropriate means to achieve a certain end. That, I call technology and nothing else. My personal interest in technology is not simply the use of technology as mass-production and efficient and economic use. Rather, I like to extract the spirit of certain materials by joining the system as art. I am interested in the art of technology but the manner in which I do it is very personal."[7]

Maki's career reveals the technological state of Japan during various time periods, both in design terms and in the use of materials and technologies, and demonstrates the ability of the Japanese architect to work with advanced technologies while maintaining a human scale and relationship. His perception of the role of technology as both the context

of operation and the means to achievement has been consistent throughout a career that bridges the extraordinary spectrum of Japan's post-war love affair with technology. At first, technology in the post-war years was seen as the panacea that would provide the means to restore Japan to a strong economic position, and at the same time revive status and respect. With this came vast technological progress bringing ecological destruction in its wake. Notable among the exploits were the major engineering works such as the building of the expressway system Tokyo – Nagoya – Osaka, and the opening of the Tokyo – Osaka express railway in 1964. Next came the disillusionment of the 1970s as the price paid became evident in the cities and the countryside. Then, the forward thrust of Japan into electronics gave it a leading position in world industry. With this came the electronic revolution in the lives of the Japanese. Following this was the boom economy and the later collapse.

In all these phases of technological change Maki responded by adapting a realistic position and accepting the time as the context for his work. The architecture rationally responded to both the state of technological advance and the conditions that it generated. But most

important was the place of technology in society. Maki writes, "The urban designer stands between technology and human need and seeks to make the first a servant, for the second must be paramount in a civilised world."[8]

Background

Maki recalls well his childhood admiration for the new machines and the ships that were at that time commonly seen in Tokyo Bay. The dynamic of the Tokyo train system would have been but a part of the normal structure of the city. Yet the wonder and power of technology as a natural part of the evolving pattern of life enthralled him then, and has continued to underlie his perception of possible architectural performance. He has been less concerned with expressing technology as such than with recapturing a nostalgic sense of childhood awe about the miracles of technology. In his early years, networks of electric information technologies were already breaking down the isolation of the Japanese nation, with the average citizen then able to tune in by radio to world events, but the structure of the city was not, as yet, greatly affected by these innovations. Lighting of the city was minimal. Tokyo was yet to receive its garlands of dazzling neon that transforms it into a dancing kaleidoscope by night.

With regard to advanced technologies, the position of post-war Japan was radically different from that of the Western world. Although certain technological advances had been taking place over more than a century, Japan, still in somewhat protected isolation, experienced a sudden impact of the industrial technologies of both war and peace. Yet despite this, Japan grasped what technology offered in its post-war recovery. In Tange's research laboratory Maki was introduced to the most progressive forum for technical exploration of architecture and urban structures in the country. Notably, Tange pioneered the application of Western materials and technologies, particularly concrete construction, to Japanese trade and building practices, deriving his aesthetic primarily from the later works of Le Corbusier. His dramatic upswirling stadia in Tokyo captured the spirit of the economic recovery of the 1960s and testified to the vast steps achieved in the technological and design fields. This was the period of the radical thinking of Metabolism, and progressive architecture was directed towards large-scale change. Precision in jointing and refinement of detail had little place in the agenda of the avant-garde architect's office. The aesthetic was that of Brutalism with the revealed construction materials and the functional parts of services and structure disclosing the wonders of these new technologies. Although television was available, electronic technologies were yet to be recognised for their invasive and transforming power, and the urban proposals from Tange's laboratory show little consideration of forces such as media technology in the shaping of the society and therefore the city.

Notwithstanding the ability of the Japanese to rapidly adapt new ideas and things to their needs, the materials of steel and concrete initially proved difficult to master. Maki's first experiences in the laboratory of Tange would have revealed very well the limitations of the construction industry at that time. Heroic imagery characterised Tange's early work, but in some instances the level of construction was not up to the task. Further, the notion of permanence, with the attendant need for maintenance, combined with the difficulty in Japan of conceiving of a public realm, resulted in even some of the most distinguished of the early concrete buildings deteriorating rapidly and presenting inhospitable settings and surfaces.

In his studies in the United States Maki was further exposed to advanced Western technologies and the rationale of mass-production. In these programs the machine and the new materials retained their fundamental role in the formation of architectural theory, providing the basis for both structure and expression. Maki's Steinberg Arts Center, 1957, for Washington University, however, was a moderately reserved building, but shows the inventive application of technology in the prefabricated folded plate roof of both the first and second storeys of the major volume. This was the time of his involvement with the Metabolists' projects which, despite their organic inspiration, relied for their realisation on the most advanced Western technologies and the growth of industrialisation in Japan. While Maki's work expressed the industrial processes it employed, it did not embody the mechanistic imagery of the more radical projects, such as those by Kurokawa and Kikutake. Further, Maki shortly abandoned this position. Nevertheless, in the following decade his projects, with those of Tange and the other Metabolists, were collectively viewed as represen-

Toyoda Memorial Hall, Nagoya University, Nagoya, 1962.

tative of the values of the industrial boom of the 1960s.

Early practice

The late 1950s were busy years for Maki with his time spent between teaching and designing in America, travelling, and designing in Japan. Concrete was Maki's favoured material for his first buildings, and he has persisted with its use where appropriate. His first Japanese building, Toyoda Memorial Hall at Nagoya University, 1962, is a Brutalist sculptural building of off-form concrete that introduced a mode of pouring on smooth-surfaced tongue-and-grove cedar formwork. This gave a much smoother finish than the board-marked finish of what was known as "Japanese concrete". This early project was among those undertaken with Takenaka Corporation.[9] Following his 1962 visit to the University, J. M. Richards wrote, "Designed by a young architect, Fumihiko Maki: in fact his first job. He was in

Tange's office and is now in America − teaching at Washington University",[10] and "... the building is all exposed grey concrete, precise in finish and admirable in colour. ... Inside, beautifully finished in grey concrete too, and well-used natural timber."[11]

Seen against the reserve of Steinberg Hall, the Toyoda Hall is startling in the vigour of both the urban character of its gesture on the axis of the campus, and in its sculptural massing. The newly released energy of Japanese architecture is evident in its confidence − Maki had learnt well from the spirit of the pioneer, Tange. But even in this early building there is a refinement in Maki's work not evident in Tange's or Mayekawa's concrete buildings of the time, or in those of Maki's peers, such as Kikutake, or even the later buildings on Kyushu of the younger Isozaki. It would seem that at Nagoya University Maki was working with both of the expressive poles of modernism, the restrained planar modelling

The National Aquarium, Okinawa, 1975.
Structural isometric.

of De Stijl and the sculptural massiveness of the late Le Corbusier. For all of its elegance, Toyoda Memorial Hall is a tough building, employing concrete technology for spatial and sculptural ends, and rejoicing in the stark aesthetic of the "brute" exposed surfaces of construction and modern services. It is the first of Maki's "portal" buildings, with a large roof supported on ferroconcrete pylons, covering positive and negative volumes of equal value in the appearance and experience of the building. Here, as in so many of his later buildings, outer spaces turn imperceptibly into inner spaces.

The approach and language present in the Toyoda Memorial Hall provided the framework for the buildings of the late 1960s and early 1970s that followed, such as the Rissho University Campus, the Kanazawa Ward Offices, the Senri New Town Center and the Mogusa Housing Estate, Tokyo. But Maki's work continued to be exploratory in its introduction of new materials, such as glass blocks and steel at the Osaka Sports Pavilion and the Tsukuba University Central Building, Physical Education and Art, and experimental structures as at Senri New Town, described as consisting of "three concentric elements – the inner core, the outer core and the peripheral frame. It is unique in the way it resists lateral forces. Lateral forces are resisted by an inverse pyramid of walls and floors anchored at the inner core in the basement."[12]

Maki's work continued consistently along such hard-line Brutalist tracks until the commission in 1971 for the Toyota Kuragaike Memorial Museum and Guest Pavilion. Here Maki's use of concrete is even more refined and the character is softer and more intimate. The commission for this pavilion coincided with the dramatic swing in Japanese values and sensibilities that followed the technologically demonstrative Osaka Expo of 1970. Although Maki did not personally participate in the design of Expo '70, nor in the politically charged revolutionary events of the time, he could not have escaped being affected by the swing of sentiment against the symbols of progress that the advanced technological building represented. Besides, the Toyota commission was generously funded, permitting a level of design attention and the use of materials far beyond that available for the previous, comparatively low-budget buildings. The Toyota Pavilion is highly reflective of its time, with an uncommon sensitivity to site and a conscious representation of Japanese handling of space, light and gardens, and of the evident prosperity of the car industry that the Memorial Museum was built to celebrate. The richness of the building's design represented the beginning of a shift in Maki's work. In retrospect, however, when seen against Stage I and Stage II of the Hillside Terraces, it is not so surprising, as the Hillside Terraces had already indicated a change from the large

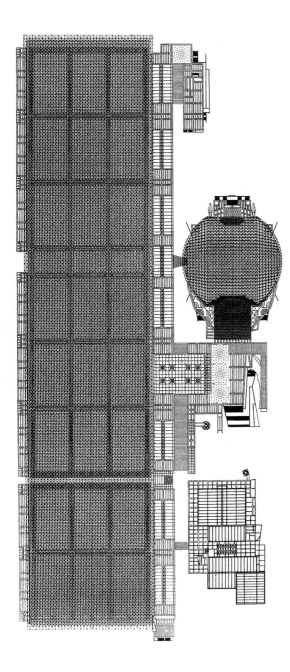

Makuhari Messe, Tokyo Bay, 1989. Structural drawing.

scale of Maki's early urban ideas to the intimacy of the urban part, and with this the possibility of detailed care in design. Maki was later to comment on this shift: "I had found that in large urban interventions there was no place for the attention to detail."[13] Not surprisingly, the move from the large to the intimate scale was accompanied by focusing on the single element, and an increased awareness of the delicacy of the local inheritance.

Prefabrication

By the 1970s Japan had sufficiently recovered from the devastation of the war to look with confidence towards a prosperous future. Japanese industry in general was expanding with the growth of the steel industry. On the negative side was the oil crisis of the 1970s and the shortage that resulted. Electronic technologies were still not sufficiently developed to have an evident impact on the use of the city, or therefore, on architecture. For the building industry both materials and structural techniques were undergoing major advances in performance, and the engineering and architectural designers were ambitious in the demands they placed on such performance. The Japanese system of vesting most

major work in the "Big Five" construction companies was firmly established, and these companies, through an internally controlled structure that provided both materials and expertise, developed very high levels of performance.

The Metabolist ideas of modular growth and flexibility of assemblage formed the basis of the design for a collaborative venture by Maki, Kikutake and Kurokawa for low-cost housing for Peru, 1973. This project was sponsored by the United Nations to relieve the housing crisis. The design used repeated concrete modular units assembled in such a way as to provide thirty-two different layouts developed to accommodate varied family needs. In all, four hundred units by twenty architects were constructed. Further early exploratory designs for the prefabrication of concrete units were executed for the Osaka Prefectural Sports Center, 1972, the National Aquarium, Okinawa, Expo '75, and Tsukuba University Central Building for Physical Education and Art, 1976.

In the 1970s Maki exploited such abilities with new realms of structural exploration including large-span structures and prefabrication techniques. The pioneering building for these avenues was the Osaka Prefectural

Prefectural Sports Center, Osaka, 1972.

Sports Center at Sakai, 1972. This was an early major structural project in which Maki worked with the master engineer, Toshihiko Kimura, with whom Maki had been associated since the mid-1960s. Kimura received his early engineering training at the University of Tokyo, and he rapidly developed an international as well as a local reputation for inventive design.[14] Apart from acting as engineer for most of Maki's buildings, Kimura was the engineer for many other challenging works of modern architecture in Japan, including Kazuo Shinohara's Tokyo Institute of Technology's Centennial Hall and Isozaki's Art Tower, Mito, 1990. Kimura's association with Maki has been long and rewarding, giving Japan some of its finest structures. It was a mutually respectful partnership, with Kimura considering Maki as having an inborn sense of structure and a profound knowledge of materials and their performance.[15]

The Osaka Prefectural Sports Center utilises huge prefabricated units spanning 21.6 meters, each consisting of tubular roof beams connecting bow-shaped trusses that create a waving surface inside and out. Due to prefabrication on a large scale, the above-grade structure was completed in only twelve days. Per-

haps most important in the realisation of this building was not the technology itself but the way in which the design relates scale and surfaces to the users and to the surrounding environment. Two significant later experiments in prefabrication, designed with Kimura, were the National Aquarium, Okinawa, 1975, and the Tsukuba University Central Building for Physical Education and Art, 1976.

The National Aquarium is monumental and heroic, with a striking use of large precast concrete arches made up of two facing sections joined by dry-jointed precast three-hinged connections, forming a noble surrounding arcade. Floor and roof slabs are also precast so that in a remote area unskilled labour could readily erect the building in a short construction time. Within the arcade is a central structural shell housing the public and service zones. The Tsukuba University Central Building was a daring undertaking with massive amber glass-block facades, consisting of 1.2-meter by 3.7-meter steel frames holding glass blocks assembled on the ground and then lifted into position on the facade by cranes. Again, as in Okinawa, dry-assembly construction was used throughout. The technology was inspired by Chareau and Bijvoet's work in

France, notably the Maison de Verre which Maki had visited. The logic of prefabrication is carried to the interior with interior partitions of cast-aluminium panels and lightweight steel studs and floors of skeleton-steel deck plates. This was a highly experimental work in the use of small glass blocks composed in large sections and developed into the scale of a very large facade. Aesthetically, the building proved to be handsome and impressive, but structurally unsatisfactory connections between materials resulted in the failure of the assemblage of the skin, and necessitated its dismantling and replacement.

Big buildings

The successful collaboration of Maki and Kimura for the Osaka Prefectural Sports Center was good preparation for the major wide-span structures of the following decades. The Fujisawa Municipal Gymnasium, 1984, the Tokyo Metropolitan Gymnasium, 1990, and the Nippon Convention Center (Makuhari Messe), 1989, involved advanced engineering structures. These metal-roofed wide-span structures challenged the limits of prefabricated technology in the fashioning of dramatic interior volumes. Their enthralling struc-

tures and gleaming roofs provide futuristic technological images. For Maki, it is the responsibility of the architect to embody in the work a representation of the present and inspiration for the future. These buildings exemplify the performance and potential of Japan at the time of their construction, through the availability of traditional craft and advanced technology, and from this rare duality Maki fashioned his work. Rand Castile writes, "Maki demonstrates that a Japanese can maintain the old qualities of the 'hand-made' structure and still push through the limits of technology. He successfully marries those 'opposites' which are the best of Japan today – the traditions of perfect craft and human scale, and an enthusiastic espousal of all that is new."[16] This is echoed in the production of the design of these buildings, which uses hand drawing and models in conjunction with computer drawings and calculations.

Fujisawa Gymnasium

In the 1970s Maki became interested in the transformation of the Japanese city from tra-

ditional buildings and relationships into a new pattern determined by what he called the "industrial vernacular".[17] In the arrangement of the new vernacular he recognised the shift into industrial production means and materials, by a certain jagged quality, and a casual arrangement of building elements and masses. This language is first explored by Maki in the Fujisawa Gymnasium, which exhibits not only the use of industrial materials but a certain tough clashing of parts, as in the roof, and of forms, as in the total composition. The distended rounded forms of Fujisawa's structure were translated geometrically into two huge arches, composed of trusses that are triangular in section and whose top and bottom arcs have different curvature, supporting the roof span. A prestressed ring runs around the top edge of the cantilevered seating and acts to absorb the movement in the roof with changes of temperature. The Fujisawa Gymnasium's steel lattice structure, utilising vaults, was followed by the much larger stadium of the Tokyo Gymnasium, with keel arches which, according to Stewart, are "more umbrella-like in

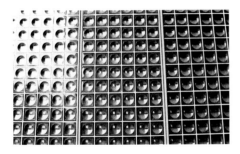

Tsukuba University Central Building for Physical Education and Art, Ibaraki, 1974.

Fujisawa Gymnasium, Fujisawa, 1984.

nature and comprise spherical, or ellipsoid, segments". He goes on, "… beneath peak-shaped skylights, the skyline becomes quadripartite, and is there seemingly composed of four valvular wings."[18]

Significant for the design at Fujisawa was the selection of stainless steel for the surface finish for the main curved roof. According to Maki, "its major advantage is its great resistance to the corrosive effects of salt air; and furthermore, its qualities of considerable luminosity, its capacity to be bent into fairly complex segments, and certain inherent qualities of scale suggested by its extreme thinness and fragility."[19] He writes that at Fujisawa the aim of the configuration and jointing of the roof segments and their texture "might then speak of the nature of steel in the same way as the grain speaks of wood, or the visible composition of minerals speaks of stone".[20] Here the folded and electrically welded jointing of the 0.4 millimetre stainless steel sheathing of the roof evidences great care in the seams and in the jointing pattern that enlivens and enriches the reading of the huge

surfaces. To achieve this resolution and refinement the supervisory team responsible for the assemblage and detail in both conception and execution worked on the site of the building throughout its construction. This is the most crafted of all of Maki's steel roofs. While models served as the major design tool, its production involved 150 preliminary drawings, 350 drawings for the contractors, and over 1,500 working and detail drawings.[21] The building of the roof of the Fujisawa Gymnasium highlights the difference between Maki's approach and that of, say, Norman Foster or Richard Rogers, where the aim is the mechanical assemblage of technological components. As he says, "Unlike Foster, I am not interested to a large extent in the assemblage of the industrial product. I am more interested in the usage and the expression of materials and space. Mine is a lower key technology."[22] To emphasise the distinction between his understanding of technology and that usually implied by the term "high-tech" Maki has coined the term "roman-tech" to better describe his work, claiming, "… one can evolve as light

and floating expression – like a flying carpet – using very developed technology that can give a sense of the romantic,"[23] and "I am at this moment more involved with the lyrical, romantic aspects of industrial society."[24]

Makuhari Messe

The conditions of the "bubble" economy provided funds for building on the one hand, yet on the other the extra availability of building jobs caused high charges for construction and materials, resulting in the need to cut amenity and quality in fixed-cost buildings. Despite this, Maki managed to achieve high performance in his structures.

Makuhari Messe, built on reclaimed land on Tokyo Bay halfway between central Tokyo and Narita International Airport, was the result of a competition held in 1986 for a major conference and exhibition center for such events as the Tokyo Auto Show. The major exhibition hall of eight identical bays 120 meters by 60 meters is energised by its swooping roof, resembling a silver bird with one short and one long wing of shining steel. This

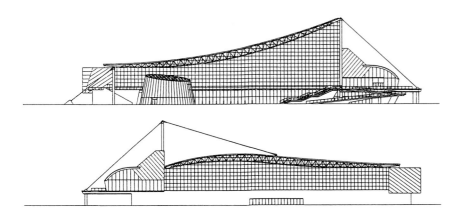

Makuhari Messe Stage II North Hall,
Tokyo Bay, 1997. Elevations.

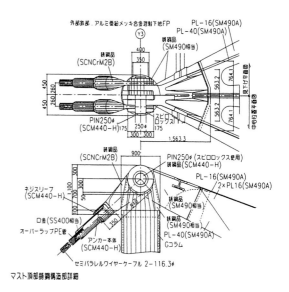

マスト頂部鋳鋼構造部詳細

Makuhari Messe, Tokyo Bay, 1989.
Upper mast: cast steel joint.

Fujisawa Gymnasium, Fujisawa, 1984.

is supported on a steel space frame of almost 10,000,000 components. The building demonstrates Maki's use of simple industrial components, such as prefabricated and in-situ concrete, space frames and trusses, but their basic elements and fixings are distinguished through an ultra-refinement of connection and detailing. With a time limit of twenty months, extensive use was made of prefabricated systems, as in the factory-produced "space" beams of the roof of the Exhibition and Event Hall and the precast concrete floor systems, but the details for assembling these prefabricated sections were all specially designed for the building. The building is demonstrative of Maki's contention that in the art of construction the architect should seek poetry in the way the building is assembled. From the sensitive combination of massive prefabrication units and quality crafted details the building achieves its special qualities. A few years after the completion of Phase I Maki was asked to

design the second stage. In this instance, rather than following the previous structural system, the roof is supported on a one-way truss that forms a wave-like form for one half of the roof and a catenary curve for the other. This shift in geometry creates a swooping overhead structure in the interior recalling the rhythm of the curved roof at the Osaka Prefectural Sports Center.

Maki never tires of searching for the expressive potential of the most advanced technologies. The laboratory roof of Triad, 2001, uses a precise section of honeycomb pieces sandwiched between two 6 mm steel plates which are separately fabricated in pieces and then joined together, and in the new School of Law for the University of Tokyo and the New Japan Rolex Building he is pushing forward explorations in the technology and expression of glass. These are buildings of contemporary relevance, with a futuristic spirit transmitted through the evident fact that

Makuhari Messe Stage II North Hall, Tokyo
Bay, 1997. Triangular truss from below.

Makuhari Messe, Tokyo Bay, 1989.
Column–roof connection.

Makuhari Messe Stage II North Hall, Tokyo
Bay, 1997. Interior.

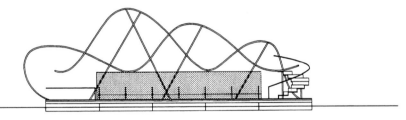

Floating Pavilion, Groningen, Holland, 1996.
Elevation.

Floating Pavilion, Groningen, Holland, 1996.

they could never have been designed or built before the advent of advanced technologies.

Electronic technologies

For the most part, the physical technologies can be harnessed and tempered, but information media and other electronic technologies belong to a different order. Beyond easy comprehension, let alone discipline, they dictate the new conditions for private and public life, to which architecture is required to respond. By the 1990s the invisible forces of electronic technologies had transformed all aspects of human existence, from private one-to-one social relationships to global economies. The Japanese architect appears to have been particularly sensitive to the new conditions affecting domestic and urban lifestyles. In Japan characteristics of the electronic age, such as impermanence, instability and ephemerality, belong to age-old ways of seeing and appreciating the world.

Delightfully descriptive of a state of mind and the state of such technologies is the Groningen Floating Pavilion, Netherlands, 1996. This building was commissioned by the adventurous Department of City Planning and Economic Affairs, Groningen, to serve as a

mobile theater sailing from point to point along the canals in the summer months. Again, it is a prefabricated structure consisting of two distinct, contrasting sections, with the light steel double spiralling frame covered with the polyester canvas membrane lightly fixed to a concrete barge 25 meters long and 6 meters wide. While basically not challenging in engineering terms, the design is a sophisticated solution capable of withstanding the strong winds that occur in the north of Holland. The delicate sculptural form with its diaphanous cover transforms each site by its appearance. Unlike the solidarity of Rossi's Theatro del Mondo in Venice that blended with, and belonged to, the Venetian backdrop, Maki's pavilion appears more like the seed fleck of a dandelion blown in from the skies to rest but temporarily on each site. Its seeming vulnerability and intangibility and fleeting state provide echoes of the times.

The marks of the maker

Despite the widespread destruction of the city, the craft quarters re-emerged in Tokyo after World War II in much the same locations as they had occupied in the past. The persistence of traditional ritual and delight in the object

and the continuance of well-tried building practices resulted in the continuing demand for specialisation and refinement in production. Craft ethics and pride in workmanship persisted with the traditional goods and practices, and the same spirit was also transferred to the use of new materials and technologies. This continues to be fostered by the structure of the Japanese building industry that allows for close collaboration between design, craft and production processes. Design changes and the refinement of production continue up to the last minute. Industry is geared to train highly skilled artisans and to adjust to "custom" design. For example, partial mass-production is possible, whereby a standard run of, say, bricks can be interrupted and provided with a particular detail for a certain number. Further, to use an expert specialist in, say, glazing for a special job, a contractor may be prepared to delay the work for a considerable time.

In architecture, a major criticism of mainstream work has been, and remains, the absence of "the marks of the maker", with a consequent sense of the impersonal and an absence of the evidence of an imbued affection in the hand-crafted good. Maki has a profound interest in materials and materiality, and this

Tepia, Tokyo, 1989. Exhibition hall.

plays an important role in his buildings. In the nineteenth century, Ruskin wrote eloquently about the virtue of hand-work and celebrated production bearing evidence of the love of creation and the skill and caring of the hands of the maker. The Arts and Crafts Movement, echoing such sentiments, pleaded for the rejection of the machine and the return to handcraft in order that both maker and receiver could rejoice in objects fashioned with human sentience. The Bauhaus, in its embracing of the machine, did not reject the Arts and Crafts belief in the joy of production for both maker and receiver, but strove to embody equal care and love in the fashioning of goods from new materials. Increasingly throughout his career Maki has become conscious of the need to overcome the negative aspects of machine production in the fashioning of materials and details, and the desire to express a new sensibility through the material quality of industrial products. He claims, "While industrial new materials must be different from old materials, like the ones you can extract from nature, the new products, glass and metal, have qualities you can extract the most out of."[25] Such a perspective is not commonly expressed regarding industrial production,

and reveals the distinctive philosophy, practice and production in the case of Maki's work. Maki talks of "humanising" modern materials such as glass and aluminium, and says that "we are still living in an age of industrial products – ranging from glass to metal to all other synthetic products – I would like to use those materials in a more sincere way to create a greater feeling of enrichment in my handling of details and small things. What I am very interested in is how we can make something similar to old buildings – that impression we get from old buildings, through the use of modern materials."[26] Inherent here is an evident concern for performance intended to overcome the cold or brutal nature of many modern building materials and to imbue production by machine with the "marks of the maker".

Elaine Scarry's book *The Body in Pain: The Making and Unmaking of the World*, which provides a sensitive model of production that is applicable to all forms of making, helps to locate Maki's position.[27] For Scarry, "making" is the process of transforming the "making up" (thought) through "making real" (production) by means of tools and materials (technology) into an artefact (building). In Scarry's

theory, the process of "making" is seen as an act of giving. The pain of work is balanced by the joy of that which is made. The act of making involves the transfer of human sentience through the artefact which is fashioned by the tool. This transfer involves the idea and the intention (theory), and the making (practice). For architecture Scarry's term "making-up" can be seen as design with the tool as "imagination" and the process as "mental imagining", with the "making real" as construction, with the embodiment of the intention and the sentience within the built object. It is both "making up" and "making real" that tempers technology. Maki tempers technology through a craft approach that humanises technological processes and materials. The key lies in the persistence of Japanese culture; Maki's work retains a sense of local place and tradition, and a transference of sentience, despite the universal and contemporary nature of the materials he uses. It manages to represent that which is local and human through that which is global and technological, but it also exhibits that which is universal and progressive. He does this through a language of abstraction using the tectonics of architecture as his tools.

In Maki's architecture the treatment of the surface and the bringing together of materials are conditioned by Japanese craft with its meticulous, aesthetic, detailed working of natural materials, and by his modern mentors in Japan, notably Tange and Kunio Mayekawa in the sculptural use of raw concrete, and by Togo Murano, a master in the handling of rich surface materials with a rare sensuality. Also of influence was his neo-Bauhaus education in America, which taught of the integrity inherent in materials in their raw state. The welcoming quality of the surfaces, the concern with shaping and pattern, the care in object form and the precision of joining bring an uncommon level of intimacy and a recognisable human scale and sense of caring to Maki's architecture. Here one might well refer to his modern Western predecessors such as Alvar Aalto, Frank Lloyd Wright and Carlo Scarpa, and in Japan to Seiichi Shirai and Murano. In writing about Murano's Peace Cathedral in Hiroshima Maki comments, "This cathedral demonstrates magnificently by its exquisite ensemble of materials that a concrete building can mature as well as any masonry or wooden building. Murano was one of the few architects who were able to endow modernist architecture, which was otherwise

beginning to show doctrinaire tendencies, with the warmth of human touch. He did this for example by using many materials and colours in a very free way."[28]

There would seem to be three major stages in Maki's career regarding the deployment of materials: first, that of the use of concrete surfaces, as previously mentioned; second, the use of ceramic cladding systems; and third, the use of metallic claddings and panels. Because of the poor weathering of the concrete in Japan's humid climate, by the 1970s Maki was frequently using tiles to clad his buildings, commonly grey ceramic tiles (notable exceptions being the New Library, Keio University, and the Royal Danish Embassy which are extensively clad with an unglazed ribbed salmon-toned tile). At the same time he extended his monochromatic palette with a highly glazed silver-grey tile juxtaposed to areas of concrete and accented by metallic fixtures and fittings. These aspects of Maki's choice of materials are a part of a general cultural interest reflected in the work of many of the major designers of the time, for example the use of a metallic skin to clothe the walls in Isozaki's Gumma Prefectural Museum of Modern Art, 1974. The use of metal claddings reached their highest expressive peak in

Maki's architecture in the great roofs of the 1980-90 period. Although the skins of the roofs dominated this time, Maki also commenced exploring the use of perforated metal materials, in order to place a screen between the building's interior and its setting. These served both to filter surroundings and to render the definition of the building indistinct. Maki's serious explorations with layered punched metals commenced at Tepia and continued to be used in his following works. At Keio University Research Center, Shonan Fujisawa, the aluminium blades are sized, angled and pierced according to their location with regard to the direction of the sun, in order to shield the enveloping glass walls and to dissolve their surfaces. Similarly, the translucent cover of the floating stage at Groningen, the flying glass overhead planes of Isar Büropark, Munich, 1994, and the total luminosity of the "cube of light" of his first Salzburg Congress Center Project indicate a search for lightness and porosity.

The soft elegance of Maki's latter architecture owes much to his selection of colours. The monochromatic range of greys of the hard materials, the steel, the concrete and the tiles, is tempered by the soft honeys and browns, mostly contributed by natural timber panels,

Hillside West, Tokyo, 1998. Facade pipe screen composition.

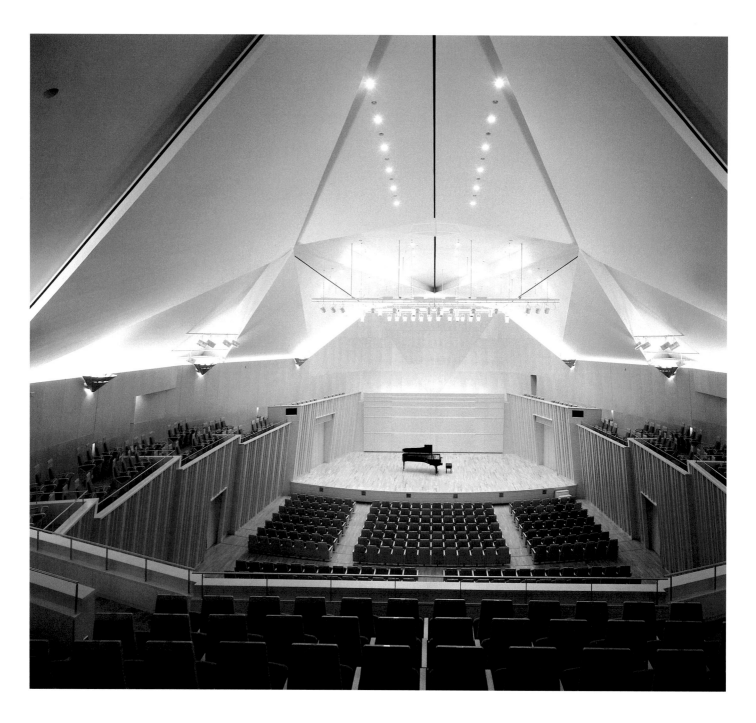

Kirishima International Concert Hall, Kagoshima, 1994.

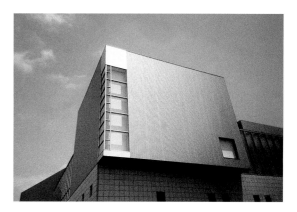

Tokyo Church of Christ, Tokyo, 1995.
Concrete detail.

Natori Arts Center, Natori, 1997.

floors and finishings. The softness of the browns balance the crispness of the whites and greys. The combination of such colouring, and the harmonies of hard and textured surfaces, owes much to Kahn, but also returns again to traditional Japanese buildings.[29] The use of light, natural timber appears in many of his projects, starting with the Toyoda Memorial Hall but is increasingly evident in the YKK Guest House and most of his following work; it is delightfully seen throughout the Tokyo Church of Christ, 1995, the main spaces of the Kirishima Concert Hall, the Natori Performing Arts Center, 1997, in wooden lattice screens behind the glass of the main facade in the Toyama International Conference Center, 1999, and it gives a sense of warmth and restfulness in the waiting room at the Kaze-no-Oka Crematorium. The first-floor lobby of the student center, Helios Plaza, at Fukuoka University, 1996, provides one of Maki's most serenely elegant interiors, where finishes, fittings and lighting fixtures combine with a cool minimalist consonance of silver, grey, and natural timber. Kirishima Concert Hall is one among several of Maki's major volumes defined by beautiful, shaped ceilings. At Kirishima the white plaster board appears to

be formed by folding as in the Japanese paper art, *origami*.

The play in the use of materials is also seen in the transition from one material to another. Carver, writing on traditional buildings, states, "The conjunction of contrasting materials, elements, or forces was a vital source of expression. Each element, each material has its own existence stated clearly yet always with a sense of value beyond itself − of the spiritual emanating from the material and the universal reflected in the particular."[30] The Guest House at Keio University, Shonan Campus, 1994, is a precise and polished building, crisp in its machine-like precision, and exploiting subtle material change within a monochromatic palette, such as smooth concrete surfaces from soft mixes off plywood forms, to board-marked drier mixes, to smooth steel panels. Delicate transitions are created simply by different treatments of the surface of the same material, like the concrete in the Tokyo Church of Christ and polished bands in the marble of the internal walls of Spiral that gently articulate the wall surface. Other transitions come from the same material but in different colours, as those appearing under the shifting nuances of light on the curved shapes

of the grey tiles at Sandoz Pharmaceutical Research Institute, Tsukuba, 1993, and their graded change over three colour tones as they move across the surface of the building. Bolder compositions combine the balancing of form and material, as at the Kanagawa University Auditorium, Yokohama, 1996, where a wedge-shaped concrete podium fits with the boundaries of the site, and is caped by the curved aluminium-clad form of the auditorium itself. Similar uses of materials to emphasise various parts can be seen at the Natori Arts Center, where ceramic tiles, glass and stainless steel panels sheath the individual masses of the composition.

Texture too plays its part, as Carver points out, with reference to traditional building: "Texture, moreover, provides one of the basic clues to scale and the added depth of close-range visual interest."[31] The juxtaposition and jointing of materials is one of the major building arts of Japanese design. This is well understood by Maki, who writes, "What endows the surfaces, both interior and exterior, of traditional Japanese architecture with a powerful expressive quality is not any iconic feature but the way in which different materials are brought together or are articulated."[32]

Dentsu Advertising Building, Osaka, 1985.
Facade detail.

Detail

To Maki, the architectural detail needs to perform major roles in modern architecture, and he explores the possibilities of an approachable abstract aesthetic through its expression and refinement. He writes that "modern architecture, having rejected ornament, leaves an unbearable void if shorn of details and a sense of material, no matter how expressive its forms,"[33] for "details restore the materiality that was lost – the materiality that people always expect and indeed demand of architecture when viewed from close distance."[34] Detail is seen to impart rhythm to the building, and is viewed as crucial to the understanding of scale and to allow the building to be read from the far and middle distances and from close up. So scale to Maki has to do not only with refinement at small scale but with the suitability of the detail to the building and the means of fabrication.[35] Maki celebrates the figurative power that details assume in the abstraction of the planes and forms of modern architecture; however, again unlike Foster, in Maki's work the detail is not important for its own sake, but rather contributes to the effort to make harmony. As Bill Lacy writes, "Whatever one touches, or wherever one's eye falls,

there is the feeling that no piece, however small, has been given less attention than the larger more important aspects of the building."[36] Exemplifying this care is the Dentsu Advertising Building, Osaka, 1985, where the subtle variation in the aluminium sheeting of the facade delineating the distinction between the horizontal and vertical members is a prelude to the rich detailing of the interiors, with all parts, including screens, paneling, hardware and light-fittings, designed by the architects. The level of attention and the totality of the design make the Dentsu Building the most lavishly finished of Maki's buildings since the Toyota Guest House. Koji Taki comments that "Maki has concentrated intensely on details. Indeed the entire Dentsu Building might be described as decorative. The result is an elegance behind which one senses a fully developed culture. This ... is achieved to the maximum extent possible by the means of outer surfaces. To produce this effect in a building as large as this is, I believe, unprecedented. The building is not decorated but is decoration in its entirety."[37] But Maki's *pièce de résistance* in materials and detailing is the later Tepia.

In 1991 Maki published a book entitled *Tepia: Details by Maki and Associates,* acknowl-

edging the special place of Tepia in Maki's repertory.[38] Tepia is a lavish jewel of material refinement in every sense, built of glass, platinum-finished aluminium panels, glass blocks, perforated metal panels and steel trim, and also with polished marble and granite floor slabs.[39] Further, Tepia is a pure intellectual building and, like many of Maki's buildings, refers back to the Modern Movement. Its roots in the De Stijl movement have already been observed, and the glass blocks, as in the cylindrical entry doorway, once again cannot help but recall both Pierre Chareau's Maison de Verre and the diffused light of the shoji screen. The building appears faultless in its craftsmanship, which is evident everywhere, from the window screens, to the hand railings, to the jointing of the panels of the skin. It was built to serve as a kind of museum of Japanese advanced technologies, with exhibition halls, conference rooms, a library and consultation rooms, and a restaurant, and was generously funded by government sources and sponsored by private industry. As Makuhari Messe celebrates Japan's prowess in the manufacturing industry, Tepia celebrates the same level of advancement in information and media technology. With all of its progressive technical

materials and sophisticated services and techniques, it is the most difficult of all Maki's buildings to come close to. There is a sense of perfection in Tepia that instils it with an icy distance, in contrast to the more textural warmth of Spiral.

The expressive use of detailing continues in all of Maki's work. Not only is detail decorative and descriptive of the tectonics but it is often charged with sensuous tactility, as with the elegant handrail to the principal stair in the National Museum of Modern Art. The potential for emotive readings also is often present, as with the weeping mortar joints at the Kaze-no-Oka Crematorium. In the subtlety of handling of detail Maki transforms traditional effects to some new modern purpose, as seen in the transformation of the light passing through the traditional rice-paper screens of the *shoji* into the glowing transmission of light through the splendid glass wall of the sanctuary of the Tokyo Church of Christ, which ensures both the distribution of light and its diffusion.

Clearly the pursuit of advanced developments in the selection of materials and the production of architecture carries economic penalties, but Maki explains: "In the case of

the YKK Research Center there happened to
be certain products, for example corrugated
aluminium panels and honeycombed panels,
which they wanted to promote, and therefore
we worked with them from the beginning. So
although the cost might have been considerable by having them on the outside they could
use the building as a kind of advertisement. In
the case of Tepia the building is a composite
of a number of architectural products from different manufacturers. But again, we suggested by going to extremes of sophistication,
although the real cost might be high, they
could demonstrate those in the kind of building where the public exposure would be
great."[40]

Tokyo Church of Christ, Tokyo, 1995.
Sanctuary wall.

Tepia, Tokyo, 1989. Screen connection.

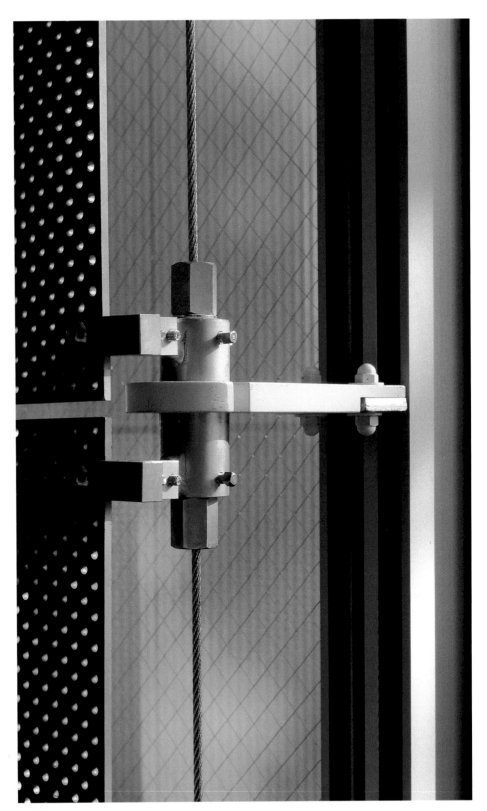

Technology to Maki is a tool to be tempered. As he says, "The use of advanced structural technology and of refined contemporary materials as finishes offers new possibilities for creating rich spatial and formal expressions. A subtle yet sumptuous ambience can be introduced in these spaces through sensitivity to material detailing."[41] Structural technology is exploited for the fashioning of space, electronic technology is used for the calculation of structure and the modelling of form, and detail becomes the decoration and giver of scale. With their involving materiality, Maki's buildings are profoundly engaged with the sensory experience. Their materials are appealing, inviting to the touch.

Notes

1 Fumihiko Maki, "Notes on collective form ", *The Japan Architect,* 16, Winter 4, 1994, p. 256.

2 Martin Heidegger, *Being and Time* (trans. John Macquarie & Edward Robinson), Oxford, Basil Blackwell, 1962.

3 Kishio Kurokawa, *New Wave Japanese Architecture,* London, Academy Editions, 1993.

4 Conversation with Maki, Tokyo, 1995.

5 Fumihiko Maki, *Investigations in Collective Form,* St Louis, The School of Architecture, Washington University, 1964, p. 22.

6 Fumihiko Maki, "The public dimension in contemporary architecture", in A. Munroe (ed.), *New Public Architecture: Recent Projects by Fumihiko Maki and Arata Isozaki,* Catalogue for exhibition, New York, Japan Society, 1985, p. 18.

7 Conversation with Maki, Tokyo, 1995.

8 As quoted in "...about Fumihiko Maki", media kit announcing the 1993 Pritzker Architecture Prize Laureate, p. 9.

9 *The Japan Architect,* September 1960, gives credit as "Design Section of Takenaka Construction Co. Fumihiko Maki, architect in charge". Maki did not open his office until 1965. In *Architectural Review,* September 1962, p. 185, in an article "Japan 1962", J. M. Richards remarks that the commission for the Toyoda auditorium at Nagoya "was first given to the Takenaka contracting firm and passed by them to Maki, who has a family connection with the firm."

10 J. M. Richards, *An Architectural Journey in Japan,* London, The Architectural Press, 1963, p. 120.

11 Richards, *An Architectural Journey in Japan,* p. 127.

12 Maki and Associates, unpublished document.

13 Conversation with Maki, Tokyo, 1975.

14 He was invited by Jørn Utzon to collaborate on the design of the Sydney Opera House, but had to decline. Conversation with Toshihiko Kimura, Tokyo, 1995.

15 Conversation with Toshihiko Timura, Tokyo, 1995.

16 Rand Castile, "About Maki and Isozaki and this exhibition", in Munroe (ed.) *New Public Architecture: Recent Projects by Fumihiko Maki and Arata Isozaki,* pp. 8–9.

17 Riichi Miyake provides an interesting essay in "Industrial vernacular", *The Japan Architect,* 62, 2 (353), February 1987, pp. 10–13.

18 For an excellent description of the construction of the roofs of these stadia in comparison with Tange's buildings at Yoyogi see David B. Stewart, "Lightness", *The Japan Architect,* 65, 8/9 (400/401), August/September 1990, pp. 29–30.

19 Fumihiko Maki, "Technology and craftsmanship", *World Architecture*, 16, 1992, p. 42.

20 Fumihiko Maki, "The roof at Fujisawa", *Fumihiko Maki: Buildings and Projects*, New York, Princeton Architectural Press, 1997, p. 157.

21 Yasuo Watanabe, "L'elmo del guerriero" (The warrior's helmet), *Spazio e Societa*, 8, 31/32, September – December 1985, pp. 24–35.

22 Conversation with Maki, Tokyo, 1995.

23 Conversation with Maki, Tokyo, 1995.

24 Interview "To offer unforgettable scenes: a discussion with Fumihiko Maki", *The Japan Architect*, 62, 3, March 1987, p. 68.

25 Conversation with Maki, Tokyo, 1995.

26 Fumihiko Maki, Interview, "The making of a modernist", *World Architecture*, 16, 1992, p. 39.

27 Elaine Scarry, *The Body in Pain: The Making and Unmaking of the World*, New York and Oxford, Oxford University Press, 1985.

28 Fumihiko Maki, "Introduction", in Botond Bognar, *Togo Murano: Master Architect of Japan*, New York, Rizzoli, 1996, p. 20.

29 Maki especially admired the timber panelling of Kahn's Salk Institute.

30 Norman F. Carver, *Form and Space of Japanese Architecture*, Tokyo, Shokokusha, 1955, p. 45.

31 Carver, *Form and Space of Japanese Architecture*, p. 72.

32 As quoted in James Stewart Polshek, "The art of building: Recent projects by Fumihiko Maki and Arata Isozaki", in Munroe (ed.), *New Public Architecture: Recent Projects by Fumihiko Maki and Arata Isozaki*, p. 12. Maki made this comment in the context of a discussion on the Fujisawa Gymnasium.

33 Fumihiko Maki in *Fumihiko Maki: An Aesthetic of Fragmentation*, Serge Salat and Françoise Labbé (eds.), New York, Rizzoli, 1988, p. 12.

34 Fumihiko Maki, "Introduction", *The Japan Architect*, 65, 8/9 (400/401), August/September 1990, p. 9.

35 Maki, "The public dimension in contemporary architecture", p. 18.

36 Bill N. Lacy, "Homage to the light", *Space Design*, 1 (256), 1986, pp. 68–71.

37 Koji Taki, "Architects and builders: The work of Fumihiko Maki and Tadao Ando", *The Japan Architect*, 58, 11/12 (319/320), November/December 1983, p. 57.

38 Fumihiko Maki, *Details by Maki and Associates: Tepia*, Tokyo, Kajima Publishing Co., 1991, p. 7.

39 Martin Spring, "Japanese roman-tec", *Building*, 4, January 1990, pp. 49–58.

40 Conversation with Maki, Tokyo, 1995.

41 Fumihiko Maki, "Space, image and materiality", unpublished notes for a lecture, February 1995.

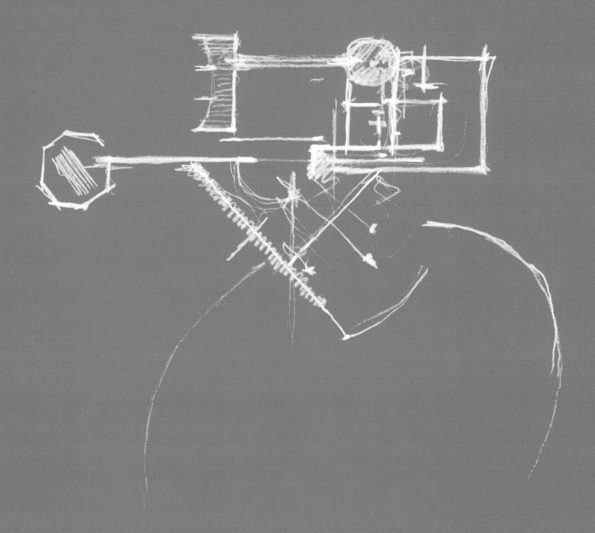

Kaze-no-Oka Crematorium: Movement diagram.

6 Space: Movement Spaces

Zen affirmed the reality of immediate experience and yet declared its indivisibility from a present defined as "the moving infinity" – its oneness with life in eternal flux. Space was felt to be the only true essential for only in space was movement possible. Space was the universal medium through which life moved in constant transformation, in which place and time were only relative states. Change was something that could not be arrested but only guided – a movement through space that could not be confined but only directed.[1]

Among the major challenges facing the architect in the twenty-first century is the need to accommodate the dynamic of the times without losing the traditional anchoring role of architecture. Contemporary technologies, notably electronic information technologies, have caused radical shifts in the current appreciation of the space-time relationship, giving rise to changes requiring adjustments within the architectural demarcation of space. Within this relationship, time assumes a dominating position, and space serves as its medium. Given this, architectural design can be thought of as the manipulation of space to shape experiences in time. In such architecture the experience of space through time is the only "true essential".

Considering Maki's overseas experience and international *savoir-faire*, one could say that he is the most Western of Japanese architects. The reading of his work as "Japanese" appears to derive primarily from the spatial organisation of the buildings, which, while resulting from a highly intellectual process of transformation, retains an aura evocative of traditional modes of composition.[2] Kuma has argued that "Maki's Western training is very important to him in that he picked up the notion of continuity as the essence of modernist space, and then found the similarities between the Japanese traditional space concepts and the modernist space concepts."[3] That is, Maki's Western training has equipped him to discover the nature of Japanese space.

Maki believes, "that the spatial constructs are more powerful carriers of Japanese architectural tradition than those associated with forms, which are often derivates of wooden architecture, and that such spatial characteristics could offer broader architectural implications for our contemporary life, making self-rejuvenation easier."[4] To extend this theme, one can say that in Japanese architecture the form is from the outside world, but the Japanese spirit is what imbues the work, and the spirit is simply spirit, not form.[5] Further, Maki privileges space over function as "spaces that reflect the will of a city or society cannot be exhausted. I believe that spaces with strength and nobility can transcend function and survive on an existential level."[6]

Maki conceives of space in a bodily sense, thinking of it in terms of occupancy and physical use. He writes: "Spatial design must become a fountainhead of spontaneous, rich human events."[7] Notions of space with Maki extend from the spatial flow of the city to the singular space within the house. Through all scales and ranges of enclosure Maki's space is not static but charged with movement or potential movement, encapsulating the additive space of the *sukiya* style of traditional design, liberated by the endless space of mod-

Kenzo Tange, Cathedral of St Mary, Tokyo, 1964.

ernism. He states that, "space is always moving and sequential. We often enjoy those sequences and the experience of a journey more than the arrival at a certain point. So we are talking about the loop: you go around and come back to an original point and the journey is the total experience rather than going to find something and coming back."[8]

Maki's sense of space is conditioned by Japan, the West, and today's understanding of global hyperspace. The early works of the 1960s introduced the major themes of evolving layered and enfolded space, and the classification of spaces into particular functional areas and freely accommodating communication spaces. These constructs provide the basic concepts for Maki's later development of space sequences. In the 1970s and 1980s the moulding of both interior and exterior space became the generating point of all of his architecture. He writes: "If I had to choose, I would take an architecture that is rich in space over one that is rich in form. Once space has been created, I might try to generate form, but I

would never sacrifice the quality of space to form."[9]

In the 1970s Maki's perception of spatial possibilities was enriched by his studies on the order of the environment, and the increasing subtlety and complexity of his architecture is most evident in buildings planned along linear, horizontally-aligned sequences. Such "movement space" is given its first full expression in the Toyota Guest House, 1974, and matures with the exploration of light and darkness in the Kaze-no-Oka Crematorium, 1997. It can further be seen in the Hillside Terraces with an urban scale of movement space which flows down the hill and crosses the street to culminate in the inner plaza or *nipa* of Stage VI of this project. Later, such planning was extended further to explore the possibilities of the vertical axis.

Transition

For Japan, the defeat in the war led to the questioning of the adherence to accepted Japanese practices and an enthusiastic adoption of what were seen as superior Western ways and technologies. Isozaki writes that the defeat "turned the tide against things Japanese; incorporating traditional concepts into Japanese architecture was viewed as rightist and regressive, and there was a conscious tendency to eliminate these forms."[10] Even so, by the 1950s architects such as Mayekawa and Tange attempted with the "New Japan Style" to mediate between Western and local practices.

With the Olympic Stadia, 1961–64, Kenzo Tange harnessed the new construction technology to generate a compelling volumetric architecture derived from traditional building types. But this tough and heroic statement found visual strength in the sculptural quality of its raw concrete forms. In 1964 Tange completed the Cathedral of St Mary with a dramatic interior that developed further the spatial drama of his Olympic Stadia, but in the same building Tange heralded a new, sensuous direction by sheathing the enveloping roof with shimmering aluminium. Yet it was with Tange's massive space frame for the central pavilion of Expo '70 in Osaka that the driving push of technology of the 1960s was given its supreme architectural expression. Although preceded by, and probably inspired by, Mies van der Rohe's 1954 project for a space-framed Convention Hall, Tange's platform, with its dramatic spanning roof seeming to float overhead, provided the most dramatic built encapsulation of expansive modern space anywhere. It was an icon of Japan's mastery of Western technology and space. It was also the end of a line.

The last years of the 1960s were years of major dissent and disillusion throughout the world. The angst of the Vietnam War was just one, albeit a major one, of the sparks that lit political rebellion and student unrest on both sides of the Atlantic and Pacific Oceans. Disillusionment with the "hard" architecture of the 1960s was world-wide in extent. "Establishment" architecture was rejected by the student

Kenzo Tange, Central Pavilion, Expo 1970,
Osaka. Space frame.

Togo Murano, Kasuien Annex, Miyako Hotel,
Kyoto, 1959.

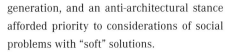

Kenzo Tange, Central Pavilion, Expo 1970,
Osaka. Space frame.

Togo Murano, Kasuien Annex, Miyako Hotel,
Kyoto, 1959.

generation, and an anti-architectural stance afforded priority to considerations of social problems with "soft" solutions.

Evident throughout Japan in the early 1970s was the increasing damage wrought by the rampant advance of industrialisation, and the attitudes that had supported the wholesale acceptance of Western directions were being called into question. Many architects sympathised with the ideas of the students' and farmers' uprisings, and the Metabolist buildings, which were viewed as representing industrialisation and the values associated with it, fell into disfavour. The country was beginning to change, and with it the form and space of architecture.

Maki's writings and designs of the 1970s show an increasing appreciation of, and empathy with, small elements and ritual, resulting in an increased sensitivity and delicacy in his work. The shift in Maki's architecture from the general to the particular arose from his increasing awareness of the inability of the designer to create individual places of delight when working in the abstract or at a gross scale. In this shift in preoccupation Maki was not alone. Precedent was to be found not only in the Japanese-inspired concrete buildings of Tange and Mayekewa but in the revival of traditional building materials and practices for modern buildings, notably with the poetic aesthetic of *sukiya* style as it was presented in work by Junzo Yoshimura and Togo Murano. Of particular significance for Maki was the architecture of Murano who had developed a

mature sukiya style before the war and in 1959 completed his influential Kasuien annex of the Miyako Hotel, Kyoto. In his 1995 essay on Murano, Maki wrote, "Sukiya is a world that involves not just vision but all the senses. Perhaps Murano's work is reassuring because he was more skilled at creating a fully tactile space."[11] Murano had also shocked the rationalists by the sensuous surfaces and lines and rich decorative materials of his contemporary office and commercial buildings and theaters, such as the Sogo Department Store, Tokyo, 1957, and the Nihon Seimei Building (Nissei Theater), 1963. In writing on the Nihon Seimei Building, Maki commented that it was "one of the first buildings to enjoy the luxury of a granite exterior finish. It heralded in that sense the end of the post-war era."[12]

So marked was the change in architectural expression from the 1960s to the 1970s that in 1971 *The Japan Architect* published a special issue on "New Generation Architects" to indicate a conceptual shift, and in 1977 the term "Post-metabolism" was coined in the same publication.[13] Following the 1978 exhibition at the Institute of Architecture and Urban Studies in New York, "A New Wave of Japanese Architecture", this work was referred to as the "Japanese New Wave".[14] Writing of the 1970s, Isozaki commented on the re-surfacing of significant Japanese themes and referred to "the increased sense of materials, the emphasis on shadows, the absence of colours, and the reintroduction of silent spaces as voids".[15] Perhaps the most dramatic shift occurred in the

approach of Isozaki himself, whose robots had been a major feature of Tange's Expo '70 central building. Isozaki's buildings of the 1960s on his home island of Kyushu had been of robust, even aggressive, sculptural off-form concrete designs, but in the 1970s he started to use soft greys and silver metals in carefully detailed claddings and softly modulated interior spaces. So Maki's work of the 1970s is expressive of the general tenor in Japan that involved a questioning of the panacea offered by technology, and an accompanying softening of the arts.

Ma, Oku:
publications on Japanese space
During the 1970s Maki continued with his teaching career, having been appointed Visiting Lecturer at the Department of Urban Engi-

Spatial order in the hilly Yamanote area of Tokyo.

neering at Tokyo University in 1968. In 1979 he was appointed Professor of Architecture there, a position he held until 1989. During these years he also travelled extensively as a visiting critic or lecturer to various universities, principally in the United States. Through this period Maki's design projects were paralleled by research studies, notably into the spatial and morphological structure of Tokyo. This work started as a group project initially funded by the Toray Science Foundation, and was subsequently published by Kajima in 1979 as *Visible and Invisible City: A Morphological Analysis of the City of Edo-Tokyo.*[16] The study presents morphological principles and the evolution of the physical spaces of the city. He followed this in the 1980s with a series of studies on the nature of the specific space constructs of *oku, meisho* and *niwa,* and subsequently published his conclusions in English both in Japanese and overseas journals.[17]

Maki's various publications on Tokyo contributed considerably to what was a highly significant and growing body of writing in the English language concerning Japanese space. While modern architects such as Wright, Taut and Gropius had reported their appreciation of Japanese space, for the most part the cross-cultural learning of the 1950s and 1960s had

primarily been from the West to Japan. An exception is found in the 1955 seminal, principally photographic, work of Norman Carver, *Form and Space in Japanese Architecture,* which explained to a Western audience the qualities of Japanese design.[18]

In 1966 a German scholar in Kyoto, Günter Nitschke, published in *Architectural Design* his research findings on Japanese space in a comprehensive article entitled, "*Ma:* The Japanese sense of place".[19] This extensive and highly revealing analysis grew out of the effort of a group of interested architects including Yasuyoshi Hayashi, Reiko Tomita and Arata Isozaki. It showed the distinct and different ways of perceiving and understanding, and therefore designing, space in Japanese culture as seen from different perspectives and in different contexts. Notably it elucidated the concept of *ma,* most simply described as "that which is between". The next significant exposure was the "Ma: Space-Time in Japan" exhibition held in Paris, New York and Rome, with the publication in English in 1979 of an article by Isozaki in *The Japan Architect* entitled "Ma: Japanese time-space".[20] These publications were complemented in 1985 by the publication of Mitsuo Inoue's historical text, *Space in Japanese Architecture,* in which he surveys

perceptions and spatial organisation in Japan through the historical periods.[21]

Whereas Nitschke's studies had embraced objects, crafts and buildings as well as town space, Maki concentrated on the layout of the street and the square. His principal observations were related to the notion of *oku,* identified by Maki as "innermost", "least accessible", "extending far back" and "a sense of depth", and *meisho* and *niwa* as distinct layers of public/semi-public space. Maki thinks of the *oku* as being enclosed, as it were, within layers as with the rings of an onion. He writes, "at the origin of the formulation of the physical spaces in Japan rests the concept of a centripetal space structure, the *oku*",[22] negating the notion of center or any other absolute value. He contrasts the *oku* space with the centrifugal space of Western cities leading to a hierarchical center. For Maki, "The center can be set by anyone concerned, and need not be apparent to others ... Innermost space as an ultimate destination often lacks a climactic quality. Instead, it is through the process of reaching the goal that drama and ritual are unfolded."[23] Carver observed that traditionally in Japan there was no sense of a Western formal hierarchy of space leading to a climax, but rather a subtle movement from dark to light,

Spatial order in the flat Shitamachi area of Tokyo.

from higher to lower, from man-made textures to natural textures, a "working outward from precision towards the vague undefined void".[24] Maki adds, "*Oku* implies something abstract and profound. It is an esoteric concept, and one must recognise that *oku* is used not only for describing spatial configurations, but also for expressing psychological depth: a kind of spiritual *oku*"[25] which "is nothing but the concept of convergence to zero".[26] The dynamic spatial movement pattern related to the idea of the uncentered, unreachable *oku* finds empathy with the Shinto notion of *nagare*, flow; the flow of life from the root of existence.

Basically, Japanese space is conceived of as having a depth composed of layers, thus introducing the idea of sequence, and, with that, the revelation of images in succession. Maki observed that space in the hilly Yamanote of Tokyo (where Maki lives) is cinematographically revealed along narrow, turning and sloping lanes, often bounded by high fences that conceal then reveal unanticipated sights. There is always that which is unknown and beyond. Contrarily, in the low Shitamachi (where Maki's office was located for most of his career)[27] regular streets are bordered by long narrow properties offering their short dimen-

sion to the passer-by. In this area "that which is beyond" is protected, not by directional change and slope as in the Yamanote, but by filtered layers of spatial depth. The sense of mystery and the sequential nature of revelation is the same, but the means of achieving it is different. Tokyo today has acquired a further spatial division and layering from the high-rise buildings that commonly line the major streets, forming deep-walled enclaves of the traditional houses and alleyways behind. Never failing to amaze are the juxtapositions within the Japanese city, and none is more striking than the spatial dialogue established by the enfolding of the small and the old behind walls of the large and the modern.

Maki's writings on space made a considerable contribution to urban theory, making available an appreciation of Japanese space concepts to a non-Japanese audience. Further, although notions such as *oku* and *ma* are not literally applied in Maki's buildings, they inform his thinking and intuitively guide the designs.

Shoin and *sukiya*

One construct of Maki's architecture relates particularly to the relationships of linked spaces that developed in Japan in the *shoin*

style. In his book *Space in Japanese Architecture,* Inoue claims that it was such architecture as developed in the Feudal Period around the sixteenth century that was particularly inventive and distinctly Japanese.[28] Inoue's observations are respected by Maki for the constructive analysis they provide of the order of Japanese space throughout history. The book's highly informative text reveals the marked changes in space demarcation and use throughout the various political periods, which show a shift from concerns with exterior composition in the Heian Period to the generation of architecture virtually exclusively from interior space in the Feudal Period. Inoue traces the evolution of the *shoin* style from the creation of more complex interior space by joining two or more rooms of differing character, to extension through addition and division. Maki mentions that the Japanese refer to such a plan as resembling a flock of wild geese.[29] Clearly such a turning lineal spatial sequence, as typical of the *shoin* style, is uncentered.

As the spaces were disposed in free arrangements, then linked by connections bent and rotated at will, the exterior form merely reflected the organisation of the interior rooms. Inoue writes that there developed

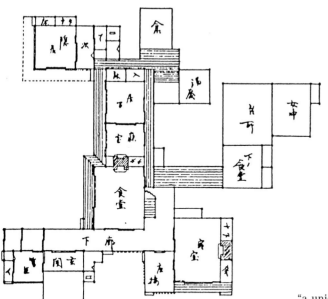

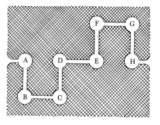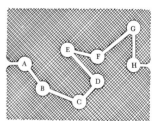

Diagram of movement spaces, from Inoue, *Space in Japanese Architecture.*

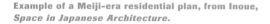

Example of a Meiji-era residential plan, from Inoue, *Space in Japanese Architecture.*

"a uniquely Japanese system of composition of interior and exterior spaces, manifest in the layout and siting of everything from gardens and individual buildings to cities".[30] This particular manner of spatial composition was based on human movement, producing what he called "movement-oriented architectural space" or "movement space", wherein "the observation of movement space ... is always postulated on the viewer's movement, whether actual or intellectual".[31] He compares the linking system of movement space to a railway diagram, as "in movement space the rooms are strung together like beads on a string".[32] The relaxed, uncentered and non-climactic spatial organisation resulting from such a loose composition leads to the *sukiya* style with its free, eclectic qualities. In his essay on Murano, Maki commented, "Sukiya is imbued with a spirit that is critical of the established forms of the mainstream and is assertive of individuality ... It is characterised by open-endedness and freedom of architectural form ... Unlike vernacular architecture, it seeks refinement as well as simplicity. It is a world, in short, of artistry."[33] This notion of open-ended incom-

pleteness is also expressed in Maki's diagrams of the city.

Within Maki's early projects, as at Rissho University, there is a clear definition of the spatial types generated in the designs. A communication space was viewed as a series of linked places for improvised activities as well as a space for movement. Such linking spaces, both static and linear, were intended to allow for chance encounters and changing use. These differing spatial and functional intentions bring to mind the distinction made in structuralism wherein a fixed support and service framework provide the stable base for individual, flexible and changing infill modules, and Kahn's "served" and "servant" spaces. Neither comparisons appear totally valid, though certainly Maki's concepts of spatial differentiation have some affinity with those of structuralism. Maki's categorisation is distinct from that of Kahn in that it is not based on material or set performance establishing different spaces, but on human activity and purpose. Also noteworthy in Maki's shaping of space is the use of the "mediating" space, which creates transitional layering of

Austrian Embassy and Chancellery, Azabu, Tokyo 1976.

spaces giving various zones of openness and enclosure, or of publicity and privacy. Such transitional layering of space is common in the *shoin* style.

Japanese thought has little problem in dealing with contradictory positions, and therefore in Japan we find spatial constructs firmly rooted in both place and history, yet essentially unfixed and temporal in nature. The Japanese understanding of life, and thus space, has always involved the ever-changing, with an understanding of uncertainty and unceasing rhythm in both the material and the immaterial. Hence, it seems predictable that Japanese architects would more easily accommodate the unpredictability of the present than would their Western counterparts, the Westerners being conditioned since Plato by two thousand years of rationalist thought. This is not to suggest that such movement spaces have not had a place in the Western architectural tradition. Of note historically is the English Landscape of the eighteenth century that also derived from Asian sources, notably from the Chinese garden. Of relevance today is the dynamism of much deconstructivist architecture, of which

the path within Daniel Libeskind's Jewish Museum in Berlin provides a remarkable example.

Movement spaces 1970s

In the 1970s Maki's concern for the space-making of architecture began to dominate his thinking, notably the processional linearity of linked spaces, and the center-less layered space-making of the *oku*.

Schools

Three schools Maki designed in the early 1970s reveal distinct spatial constructs of disparate blocks linked along spines or drawn inward to a central void. St Mary's International School, Tokyo, 1972, presents a lineal arrangement following the boundary to the street, while the Kato Gakuen School, 1972, and the Noba Kindergarten, 1974, wrap internal space in bands of visually connected rooms.

The design of St Mary's International School combines a carefully resolved facade "wall", that steps back and forth in response, in both ecological and design terms, to the street edge and the splendid zelkova trees that

line it. Wings run at right angles to the street-lining spine forming courtyards and the entryway. The school activities are housed in differentiated functional and connecting-type spaces, and their individual expressions create a lively, broken skyline and plan profile. The street alignment of St Mary's was an uncommon design for Maki in the 1970s, but it was followed in 1976 by the Austrian Embassy and Chancellery in Azabu, Tokyo, which demonstrates a related consciousness of the composition of the space of the street. In that case, Maki attempted to generate in the building the qualities of the previous street-scape which had been associated with ceremony and procession. With this in mind, he sought a solution whereby the building would be revealed slowly from a moving point of perspective.

The Kato Gakuen Elementary School was the first open-plan school in Japan. The initial division of space into functional space and communication space continues here, but the connections are centripetal rather than linear as at St Mary's. The problem was one of maintaining openness yet controlling sound, and

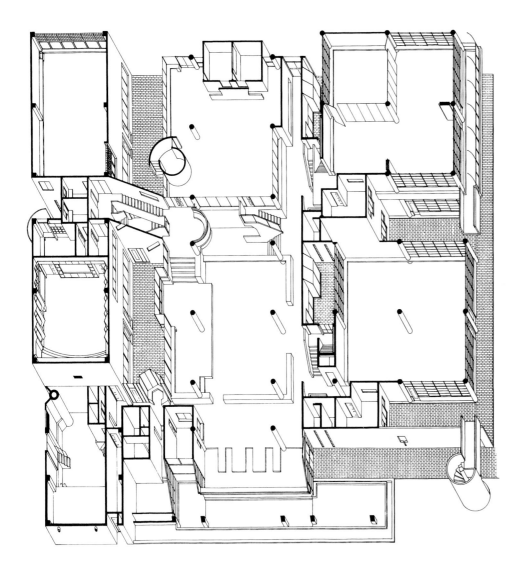

Noba Kindergarten, Tokyo, 1974. Central space.

Kato Gakuen Elementary School, Tokyo, 1972. Isometric.

providing adequate differentiation to accommodate particular activities. Typically, Maki's solution has been to articulate the class-room volumes as independent entities and then link them, in this case in a centralising manner across two central, shared volumes with connection provided by a short cross-spine. Several open courtyards and glazed walls on the inside ensure a total volumetric reading demonstrating the educational nature of the school. Noba Kindergarten belongs to the same spatial and social family as the Kato Gakuen School, consisting primarily of a major shared yet differentiated central band of spaces for the nurseries; at Noba Kindergarten this is distinguished and lit by tall and narrow vertical slits of space crowned with a skylight at either end of the central zone. There is a sense of compressed space in these buildings, which derives in part from the strong supergraphics but also from the intentionally reduced details and low ceilings, designed to

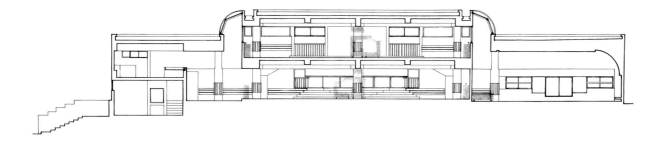

Noba Kindergarten, Tokyo 1974. Section.

accommodate the child's appreciation of size. The spatial order of the buildings, their scale, and the integration of furniture for interpretative play use by the children suggests Maki's debt to the Dutch structuralists, notably Aldo van Eyck and Herman Hertzberger.

Toyota Guest House and Memorial Hall
In Maki's previous work there was little to suggest the sensuous, spatial and temporal experience that the Toyota Kuragaike Guest House and Memorial Hall introduced in 1974. In its broad planning organisation, the rhythms and sequences of form, surface and space, the Toyota complex appears in the direct line of inheritance from the Japanese stroll or tea-house garden. The principal buildings consist of a Reception/Guest House in which to receive visitors, mainly from overseas, and a Memorial Showroom for the Toyota Company.

The complex is sited overlooking the beautiful lake of Kuragaike in the manner of a romantic villa, sinking into and reaching out towards the landscape. The experience of the building commences on the road from Nagoya as occasionally it is partially glimpsed, folded into the natural and moulded terrain of its surroundings. The close approach to the building is along a curved drive through sculptured earth forms and plantings already heralding a new direction in Maki's work. The public is provided with an entry directly connected with the Memorial Hall to the south, whereas guests enter on the north side of the building. This entry provides the first step on a processional route that leads into the guesthouse, on to the exhibition area, and eventually back to the guesthouse. The evidence of a traditional sense of form and surface is immediately evident at the guest entrance where finely finished round posts and delicate screens strongly suggest a quality and form such as might be found in a Shinto shrine. Inside, the mood and demeanour of the building are quickly established for the visitor, who is immediately confronted by a richly-surfaced, curved screening wall revealing, through a floor-level ribbon of glass walling, an internal courtyard edged with a low, narrow band of azaleas surrounding a cone of white sand. Spatially, the building is laid out as a journey involving continuous shifts of direction and level changes linking distinct, luxuriously finished rooms and passages. Wall openings and transitional zones are temptingly located in a traditional manner, to reveal selected outlooks to the surrounding gardens from strip windows at eye-level when seated, or tantalisingly small punched openings exposing glimpses of framed vistas as one moves along connecting passageways. Perhaps the major creative stroke of this work lies exactly here, in what Philip Drew describes as "Maki's brilliant circulation path with its superb orchestration of vistas and tantalising glimpses of the surrounding landscapes".[34]

The plan of the Toyota Guest House and Memorial Hall combines a varied path of weaving spaces with a controlling order imposed from a long and straight linking cross-axis edged with opposing right-angled triangular volumes to each side. Those tight geometric figures are invaded by the curves of walls and ramps. Each space, its containment, connections and visual release, has been shaped for its purpose, taking full account of furniture and furnishings, orientation and outlook. The flowing path of the spatial sequence breaks through the strict geometry, and, moving in from the garden, a pond and plantings penetrate the frame in a studied arrangement specifically designed to be viewed, in the traditional manner, from a particular room. The

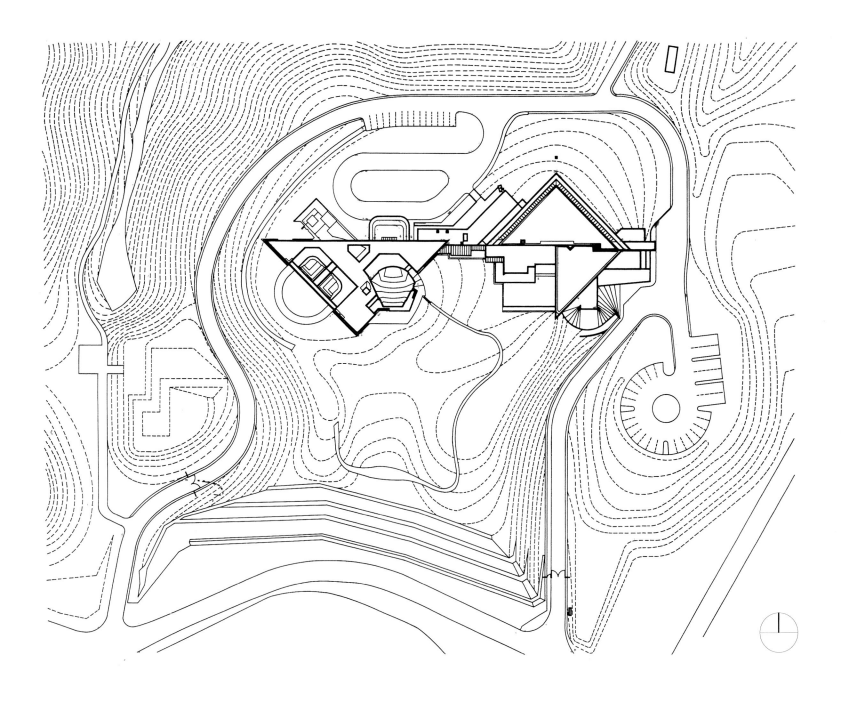

Toyota Guest House and Memorial Hall, Nagoya 1974. Site plan.

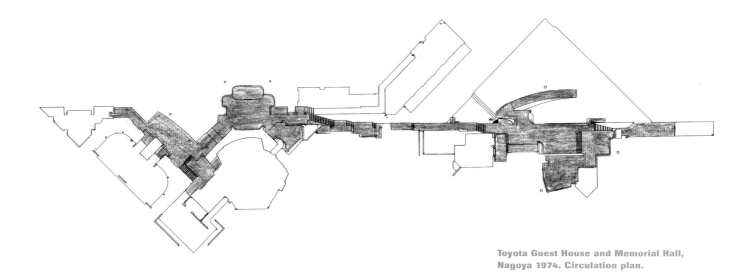

Toyota Guest House and Memorial Hall, Nagoya 1974.
Entry.

visitor is guided from the reception point, a waiting room and an informal lounge, through a transitional corridor with multiple level changes to the Memorial Hall exhibiting Toyota's history. From there the tour is reversed along a route revealing new outlooks and spaces, back to the formal lounge and dining room where the principal view, that of the lake, previously withheld, is revealed at the end of the journey. Changes of level and direction contribute to the constant revelation of new interests, and the space itself seems far greater than it really is due to the changing directions of the movement path providing shifting views of the same spaces or objects from different perspectives. It is an explicit exercise in working with a sequential temporal pattern. For an article in *The Japan Architect* Noburo Hozumi produced some amazing statistics. He calculated that the distance from the guesthouse to the exhibition hall was in the vicinity of 100 meters, that a tour of the building would cover half a kilometer involv-

ing 55 turns for a total of 3,600 degrees of turning, and all within a building of 3,500 square metres![35]

The Toyota Guesthouse and Memorial Hall stand alone in Maki's oeuvre of this time. Although he continued to develop his planning along sequential routes, other buildings do not exhibit the same degree of contrivance. Further, while he has continued to employ elegantly-detailed, rich materials, his subsequent buildings have not been enriched by such a surfeit of sumptuousness. Also uncommon for Maki at this time, and not so directly demonstrated until his work of the 1990s, is the underlying romantic design concept of the total organic integration of building, garden and setting. In addition, the traditional sources drawn on are explicit in this building, whereas in later work they are subtly sensed rather than seen. The Toyota villa appears as a reactionary building, extreme in its embracing of, and demonstration of, principles and attributes polar to those characteristic of the technological stance adopted in Japan in the previous decade. It provided an important breakthrough and liberation for Maki, and in its radical departure from prior rationalist tenets, it shocked and challenged the profession.

The National Aquarium

The National Aquarium, Okinawa, built for Expo '75, offers a contrasting example of Maki's ambulatory designs, for here a strict rectangular layout is imposed by large-scale prefabricated arched structural units defining broad and long double-level colonnades edging the perimeter of the principal structure. The building presents its long side to one of the main circulation paths of the Expo site, seeming – through its side stair and the generous monumental stepped podium at the entrance – to scoop passers-by up into the shelter of its broad, shaded arcades. To the south the pathway passes Maki's Dolphin Studio and Show Pool, which bear a studied, but

Toyota Guest House and Memorial Hall, Nagoya 1974. Corridor.

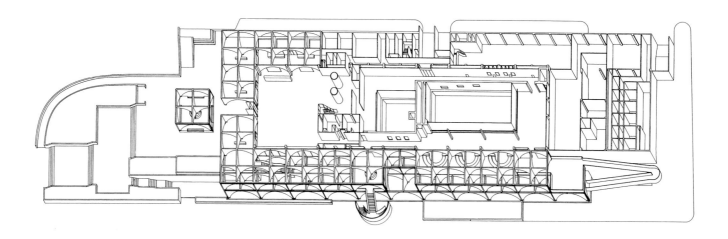

The National Aquarium, Okinawa, 1975.
Isometric.

not particularly evident, relationship to the Aquarium building.

The bright, open, hard quality of the exterior arcades of the National Aquarium, which provide views out over the blue ocean, is countered by the antithesis offered by the exhibition area with its subdued, enclosed, carpeted space. This is a strangely detached surreal space of quiet and darkness. The two huge lit tanks containing the shimmering and darting fish appear suspended in a mesmerising way in boundless darkness, with the visitor guided as much by a muted tactility as by sight. Surrounding the tanks is the path, a place of blackness wrapped around brilliance, with each adding to the intensity of the other. The effect is not unlike that experienced on entering a Gothic cathedral with the glowing windows suspended in blackness. Only in Isozaki's architecture does one find comparable spaces embodying a particular quality of darkness.

The National Aquarium consists almost entirely of movement space, along the generous shading arcades of the exterior walls and within the interior of the two major volumes of the entry foyer and aquarium proper. Both major exterior and interior spaces are places of rest as well as passage. The deep arched arcades were designed as both points of shelter and points of prospect over the blue waters of the sea. Inside, off the viewing ambulatory, dimly lit and softly surfaced seating bays offer rest and a passive viewing of the kaleidoscope of colour offered by the fish in the tanks.

Movement spaces 1980+

Maki's buildings of the 1980s and 1990s tend to be distinguished by either linear, sequentially connected spaces, as explicitly demonstrated in the earlier Toyota Guest House, or by clustered groups of spaces typically seen in the large-volume buildings, such as the gymnasiums. At this time the work also evidences a marked interest in the exploration of vertical linear sequences. The central volume compositions are surprisingly complicated in the massing of the major and subsidiary volumes and the spatial relations established between them externally. Also intricate and quite arresting are the spatial relations set up between the total complex and its setting. The frag-

The National Aquarium, Okinawa, 1975.

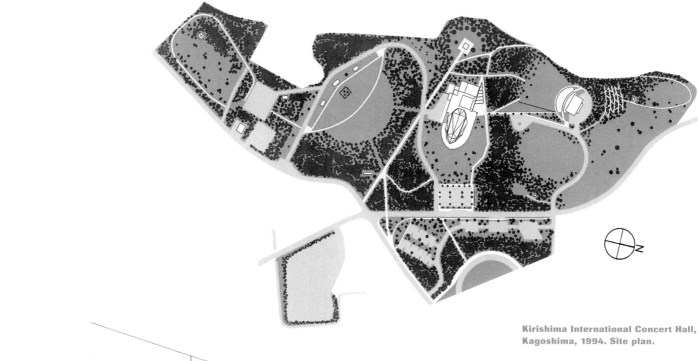

Kirishima International Concert Hall, Kagoshima, 1994. Site plan.

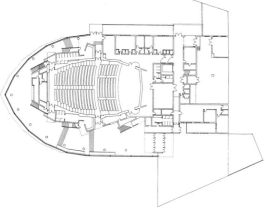

Kirishima International Concert Hall, Kagoshima, 1994. First floor plan.

mentation of the functional volume into two or more major units, as found at the Toyota complex, characterises projects of both spatial grouping patterns.

Kirishima Concert Hall

The Kirishima International Concert Hall, Kagoshima, 1994, introduced further spatial dimensions to Maki's work. Here a linear linking along a progressional path, in the manner of the Toyota Guest House, provides a circulation path revealing the volume of the building units and sequentially disclosing their particular visual connections to the dramatic surrounding mountain scenery. The approach starts at the lower carpark, climbs up the hillside towards the face of the building, sends an embracing spur path to the open auditorium on a lower terrace to the north, passes alongside the main hall, and turns 180 degrees to enter the foyer up an elegant low tier of wide stairs towards the dramatic view beyond the glass walls of the central lobby. A further 180-degree turn leads into the auditorium. The route establishes both difference and continuity. The path links exterior and interior space, while through its various materials and surface treatments it clearly defines zones of differing character.

Kaze-no-Oka Crematorium

Kaze-no-Oka Crematorium, 1996, – the name means "Hill of the winds" – is situated in a park at Nakatsu in Southern Japan. Its plan has even stronger affiliations with that of the Toyota Guest House. As Maki comments, "Both seek the sequential quality of space and evocation of human responses. The crematorium, in addition, provides the sense of depth (okuness) through controlled natural light, synthesising both direction and depth."[36]

The crematorium consists of three buildings along the sloping terrain in a large sweeping park: the brick funeral hall, the concrete

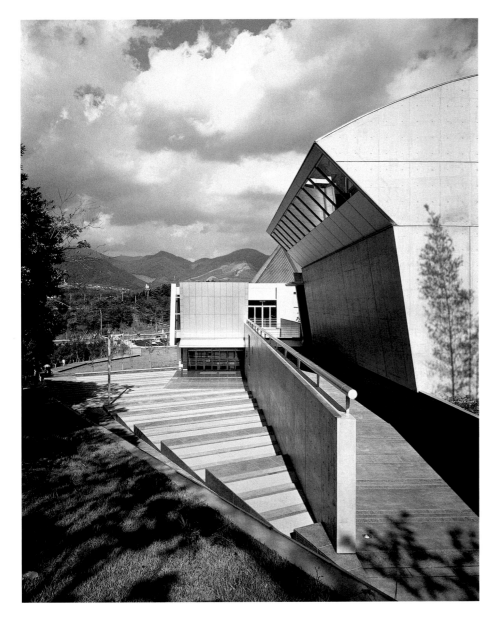

Kirishima International Concert Hall, Kagoshima, 1994.
Approach.

Kirishima International Concert Hall, Kagoshima, 1994.
Interior stair.

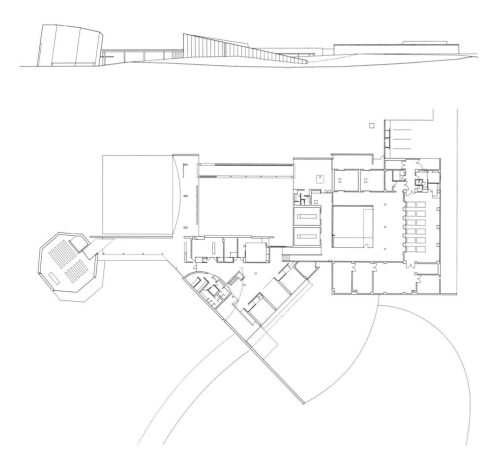

Kaze-no-Oka Crematorium, Nakatsu, 1996. Elevation and Building plan.

Kaze-no-Oka Crematorium, Nakatsu, 1996. Crematorium porch.

crematorium, and the red weathered steel waiting area and shielding wall. The building provides a summation of the spatial notions explored in Maki's work since the 1960s. This closed space of death is modulated with a sensitive refinement principally through his handling of the ritualistic path itself and through his subtle modulation of light and darkness. Nowhere is this more poignant than at the solemn place of the cremation itself where, behind the mourners, a large pool of water and open skies expand and free the spirit.

As with the Toyota Guest House, the buildings slice through, sink into, and are mounded by the land, in this instance to emphasise the abstract sculptural forms facing the park, and to give a sense of the dying returning to the earth. The total composition provides a physical and spiritual journey into the darkness of death and release to the brightness of life. The path conducts the mourners along the route connecting the rooms for the highly ritualised ceremonies. This inward searching towards spiritual depths recalls the tradition-

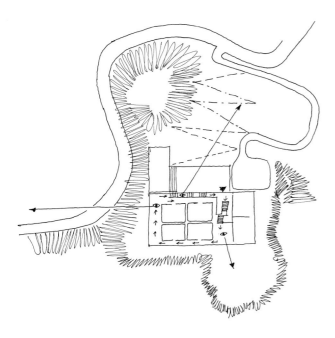

Tottori Prefectural Museum, Tottori, 1998.
Movement path.

Kaze-no-Oka Crematorium, Nakatsu, 1996.
Enshrinement room.

al approach to the Shinto shrine. The linking spaces serve not simply as connectors but as places for pause and relief from the emotional engagements of the stages of the ceremony which are conducted in pools of various degrees of darkness, relieved by slicing rays of light. The building embraces the concepts of both *nagare* and *oku* within the rhythm of the voyage through its movement spaces.

The Kaze-no-Oka Crematorium provides the most enriching spatial sequences of Maki's career. Here the gently enfolding spaces, both dignified and serene, together with the control of light, material selection, water pools and building forms, provide a symphony of experiences celebrating death and life.

Though unbuilt, the proposal for the Tottori Museum, 1998, provides another example of the continuance of this theme in Maki's architecture. At Tottori, designed for a hilltop site just outside Tottori City, the path starts at the lower level of the site and zigzags up a series of sculptural terraces to the principal platform and building. The route within the building is consciously designed to be like that of a Japanese stroll garden and to provide views of distinctly different places, the mountains, the Japan Sea and Tottori City.

Climbing movement spaces

The ambulatory sequential mode of space structuring lent itself well to diverse projects including museums, cultural centers and commercial outlets, but the extension of this organisational pattern into the vertical dimension produced some of Maki's most involving spaces of the 1980s. The modulation of space vertically and the consequent importance accorded to upward means of movement came increasingly to characterise his buildings. Early inspiration had come from the modern houses he had experienced rather than from Japanese design. The fact that the stair is an uncommon element in Japanese architecture made for a special challenge. As Hiroyuki Suzuki comments, "That was a very important thing for him, so he designed very carefully how to express such an element in Japan."[37] The stair or ramp becomes a primary object

Kaze-no-Oka Crematorium, Nakatsu, 1996. Interior courtyard.

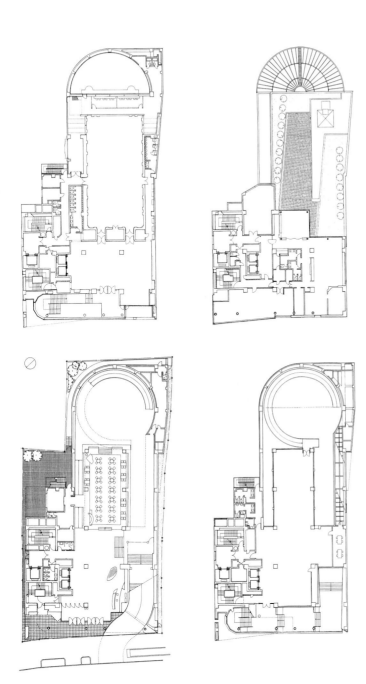

Spiral, Tokyo, 1985. Plans.

and is accorded special attention by way of location, form and detail. He writes, "To me, the staircase does not only serve the functional purpose of connecting different levels, but creates different spatial configurations."[38] The care and attention accorded stairs has given rise to many of Maki's most creative objects and experiences, and the importance accorded these elements is evident in his 1999 publication in Japanese entitled *Stairways of Fumihiko Maki: Details and Spatial Expression*.[39] In this book, Maki discusses stairs under the headings "Children and staircases", "Space surrounding stairs", "Stairs as art object", "Exchanging of scenarios", "Stairs and urban characteristics" and "The constituent element of stairs".

Although traditional Japanese buildings were primarily of one-storey construction with horizontally organised space, vertical space was occasionally deployed and was given its most dramatic expression as spiral space in the castle keeps. In these tall, commanding towers with stepped-back pyramidal outlines, the spatial experience becomes increasingly compressive, as with each higher level the interior volume decreases in size. As the available floor area decreases, the stair width becomes narrower and the going becomes steeper. Eventually the stairs begin to consume all the available space and the pull of the inescapable upward thrust of the verticality becomes overwhelming. The sense of *oku* beyond each twist, with the "ultimate beyond" at the top, is charged with a sense of the uncanny. While Maki's buildings do not involve such

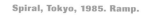

Spiral, Tokyo, 1985. Ramp.

YKK Research Center, Tokyo, 1993.
Atrium with stair.

Tokyo Church of Christ, Tokyo, 1995.
Stair and handrail.

Spiral, Tokyo, 1985. Principal stair.

extreme states of vertical movement, the sense of an upward pull towards an unknown *oku* is clearly sensed in Maki's confined buildings in the city, including Spiral, 1985, the YKK Research Center, 1993, and the Tokyo Church of Christ, 1995. As at Le Corbusier's Villa Savoye, options for vertical movement are dramatically offered.

Most explicit are the modulated vertical movement paths of Spiral which lead increasingly and temptingly inwards to the full depth of the building in plan, then upward along the sweeping ramp of the spiral and up a series of varied, enticing stairways. The alternative broad stair rising inside the street facade acts as an extension of the spaces within the building, but also as a transitional zone linking those within and without. The choice of paths offered at Spiral is also made available in the YKK Research Center. Here, a turning stair framed by freestanding green tubular steel poles is played against a smoothly rising grand stair leading to the stepped terraces of the reception and work floors. At the Tokyo Church of Christ, the movement upward towards the sacred unknown provides a transition from noisy street to inner sanctum. In this building an easy-graded stair leads upward through a series of resting and relaxing spaces that slowly release the worshippers from the stresses of the city in preparation for the experience of the service. Also thoughtful is the handrail: a steel rail for adult use, and a lower wooden rail at a height suitable for children.

The scale and pace shifts radically in the highly inventive spiral stair leading from the main hall to the loft. Here the cantilevered treads are supported by vertical riser plates between each pair of treads, and this is echoed in the handrail where vertical timber panels are similarly distributed. Stairs often feature as major elements running up the inside of the facade of buildings, serving not just for movement but for the visual enjoyment of those both inside and out. The Yerba Buena Gardens Visual Arts Center, Spiral and Tepia offer such experiences.

Although not a constrained urban building, the YKK Guest House at Kurobe, 1982, offers a further model of tightly linked vertical movement space. Here translucent screens patterned by the grid of their timber framing separate yet link the multi-level shaft of space towards the southern garden with the adjoining upper-level spaces. This freestanding shrouded central stairwell is the most haunting and seductive of Maki's vertical paths. From the foyer in which it stands, the totality of the rising space is sensed, rather than revealed, through partial disclosure. In contrast to the enclosure of the YKK Guest House stair, the path down to the waiting room at the Kaze-no-Oka Crematorium is open and clearly directional. This elemental work with cantilevered timber treads projecting from a raking, beautifully crafted sculptural concrete slab terminates gracefully in an elevated podium.

YKK Guest House, Kurobe, 1982. Central stairwell.

The play of contrasting volumes of rising space orchestrates the spatial composition of the National Museum of Modern Art, Kyoto. In this building Maki made the various stairways the demarking points of the composition, playing dramatic contrasts of mood and movement against each other. Three corners of the main balanced facades of the building are anchored by the glass shafts of the corner turrets of the escape stairs, extending the height of the building and terminating in a silhouette of pyramidal roof shapes. These shafts play against the sky as the shells of fairytale towers, both eroding the planar solemnity of the severe facade and adding a contrary, romantic note. Within the corner stair shafts, the dynamics of the spiralling path contribute to the exhilaration arising from the marked verticality.[40] The spiralling of the corner stairs is countered by the slow-flowing pace of the principal internal stair. Immediately on entry into the building one is faced, across the wide

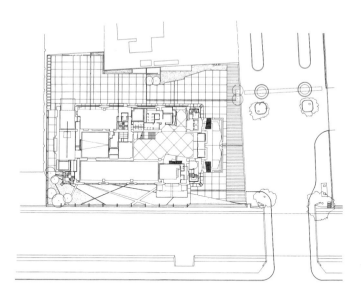

National Museum of Modern Art, Kyoto, 1986.
South facade with corner turrets.

National Museum of Modern Art, Kyoto, 1986.
First floor plan.

lobby, by the centrally located grand stair that leads to the galleries on the first floor. The stair is set apart in its own light bay, rising up to a podium demarcated by two centrally placed back-lit columns that rise the full height of the space. With the stair in the very center of the building, the sense of penetration, while there, is not as pronounced as at Spiral. The generous dimensions of this stair, the sweep of its rise, and the particular quali-

ty of the lighting entering through the roof, evoke a sense of relaxation and procession. The ceremonial nature of this stair is enriched by the refinement of the detailing and the richness of the materials. The stairs of the National Museum of Modern Art provide the extremes in the range of Maki's handling of the spaces of vertical movement, with their differences stressed as dramatic foils against each other.

Maki's interest in movement, both horizontal and vertical, is closely related to the cinematographic quality which Japanese urban scenes offer. In his view, the Japanese city cannot be appreciated from a single viewpoint as can the Western city. Rather, his special interest is strongly imbued with the daily experiences of the Japanese city that offers scenery with juxtapositions of heterogeneous constructs. Maki's writings and projects related to

movement spaces figure among his major contributions to the evolution of the shifting theoretical positions of architecture and urban design. With their ability to embrace both the dynamic of movement and the static space of occasion, they offer a flexible, open-ended means of planning, both receptive and stable.

Notes

1 Norman F. Carver, *Form and Space of Japanese Architecture*, Tokyo, Shokokusha, 1955, p. 130.

2 For example, in conversation with the author in 1996 Reiko Tomita of Team Zoo commented, "In his design with space Maki is the most Japanese of today's architects." David Stewart has claimed that "many of Maki's spaces are quite simply among the best examples of *'ma'* in modern Japanese practice". David B. Stewart, "Architecture and the beholder. Five new works by Fumihiko Maki", *Space Design*, 1 (256), January 1986, p. 115.

3 Conversation with Kengo Kuma, Tokyo, 1995.

4 Maki, letter to the author, 1 September, 1998.

5 Thoughts after conversation with Kengo Kuma, 1995.

6 Fumihiko Maki, "Complexity and Modernism", *Space Design*, 1 (340), January 1993, p. 7.

7 Fumihiko Maki, "The theory of group form", *The Japan Architect*, 45, 2 (161), February 1970, p. 41.

8 Conversation with Maki, Tokyo, 1995.

9 Fumihiko Maki, "Space, image and materiality", *The Japan Architect*, 16, Special Issue on Fumihiko Maki, Winter 1994, p. 11.

10 Arata Isozaki, "Foreword: The architecture of an open-port Japan", in Botond Bognar, *Contemporary Japanese Architecture: Its Development and Challenge*, New York, Van Nostrand Reinhold, 1985, p. 11.

11 Fumihiko Maki, "Introduction", in Botond Bognar, *Togo Murano: Master Architect of Japan*, New York, Rizzoli, 1996, p. 24.

12 Maki, in Bognar, *Togo Murano: Master Architect of Japan*, p. 24.

13 *The Japan Architect*, special issue on New Generation Architects, July 1971. See Kazuhiro Ishii, Kazuhiro and Hiroyuki Suzuki, "Post-metabolism", *The Japan Architect*, October–November 1977.

14 See Kenneth Frampton, "The Japanese New Wave", *A New Wave of Japanese Architecture: Catalogue 10*, New York, The Institute of Architecture and Urban Studies, 1978, and Kishio Kurokawa, *New Wave Japanese Architecture*, London, Academy Editions, 1993.

15 Isozaki, "Foreword: The architecture of an open-port Japan", in Bognar, p. 11.

16 Fumihiko Maki, *Visible and Invisible City: A Morphological Analysis of the City of Edo-Tokyo*, Tokyo, Kajima Publishing Co., 1979.

17 Among the essays published in English are Fumihiko Maki, "Japanese city spaces and the concept of *"oku"*. *The Japan Architect*, 54, 5 (265), May 1979, pp. 51–62; Fumihiko Maki, "The city and inner space", *Process Architecture*, 20, 1980, pp. 151–163. (This article was translated from "Nihon no toshi Kukan to *"oku"*, in *Sekai*, December 1978, published by Iwanami Shoten; the English text was reprinted from *Japan Echo*, VI, 1, 1979.)

18 Carver, *Form and Space of Japanese Architecture.*

19 Günter Nitschke, "Ma: The Japanese sense of place", *Architectural Design,* 3, 36, March 1966, pp. 116–154.

20 Arata Isozaki, "Ma: Japanese time-space", *The Japan Architect,* February 1979, pp. 69–80.

21 Mitsuo Inoue, *Space in Japanese Architecture* (trans. Hiroshi Watanabe), New York and Tokyo, Weatherhill, 1985.

22 Fumihiko Maki, "Japanese city spaces and the concept of *'oku'*", *The Japan Architect,* 54, 5 (265), May 1979, p. 52.

23 Fumihiko Maki, *Selected Passages on the City and Architecture,* internal publication of Maki and Associates, Tokyo, 2000, p. 26.

24 Carver, *Form and Space of Japanese Architecture,* p. 178.

25 Maki, "Japanese city spaces", p. 53.

26 Maki, "Japanese city spaces", p. 59.

27 He continued to practice there until he moved to Hillside West in the Yamanote part of Tokyo in 1998.

28 Inoue, *Space in Japanese Architecture.*

29 Conversation with Maki, Tokyo, 1995.

30 Inoue, *Space in Japanese Architecture,* p. 5.

31 Inoue, *Space in Japanese Architecture,* p. 147.

32 Inoue, *Space in Japanese Architecture,* p. 145.

33 Fumihiko Maki, "Introduction", in Botond Bognar, *Togo Murano: Master Architect of Japan,* New York, Rizzoli, 1996, p. 5.

34 Philip Drew, "The non-assertive architecture of Fumiko [sic.] Maki: From form making to place shaping", *Space Design,* 6 (177), June 1979, pp. 68–73.

35 Noburo Hozumi, "Colorful spatial experience – Toyota Kuragaike Commemorative Hall", *The Japan Architect,* 50, 4 (219), April 1975, pp. 49–50.

36 Maki, letter to the author, 1 September, 1998.

37 Conversation with Hiroyuki Suzuki, Tokyo, 1995.

38 Maki and Associates (eds.), *Stairways of Fumihiko Maki: Details and Spatial Expression,* Tokyo, Shokokusha, 1999. (Unpublished English translation by Yasu Watanabe, Preface, p. 2.)

39 Maki and Associates (eds.), *Stairways of Fumihiko Maki: Details and Spatial Expression.*

40 Gropius and Meyer's glass stairwell for the Cologne Exhibition of 1914 provides an evident prototype.

ELEVATION SECTION

- NOBORI
- YAGURA
- KIYOMIZO

Image of a fragmenting city.

7 City: The City in Motion

In 1971, Maki visited Australia for the "Consequences of Today" conference in Sydney. There he spoke of the problems in Japan: "Today Japan more than any other nation faces a serious conflict between technological-economic progress and the preservation of environmental quality." He pleaded that in the future the "potential of planning must be directed towards restoring the city to be a more human environment",[1] and that the city must provide "an intensive, personal territoriality and spatial identification".[2]

Maki's concern for the Japanese city was not ill-founded. By the 1970s what was called the Pacific Coast Belt or the Tokaido Megalopolis represented one of the largest and fastest growing urban conglomerations anywhere. Articles such as "Megalopolis in Japan: urbanism as a way of business" by Shunichi Watanabe and Satoshi Morito, and "Some definitions of megalopolis in Japan" by Catharine Nagashima, drew attention to the need for better management and control in order to ensure quality of life for the inhabitants.[3]

Generally, planning in Japan in the 1950s and early 1960s appears not to have been grounded in public concern but in continuing expansion and profit. A rapid increase in the population and the division of households had occurred since 1955, and the Shinjuku sub-metropolitan area plan was approved in 1960. The freeway system was planned in the 1950s and published in 1953 as "Basic Policies for Expressways in City Planning of Tokyo". The 1960s witnessed the first of the highrise buildings and the extraordinary rise in land prices everywhere. In 1969 the green zone policy was abandoned under the pressure of land for housing, and the situation worsened. The deteriorating condition of the capital and remedial measures were spelt out in regular reports published by the Tokyo Metropolitan Government.[4] Atmospheric pollution was among the most pressing problems, and was dramatically highlighted by the images of police on traffic duty wearing protection masks. The 1971 Government report *Tokyo Fights Pollution: An Urgent Appeal for Reform* graphically spelt out the history of the

growth of pollution of all kinds in the city. The later 1977 report *Tokyo Fights Pollution* although reporting progress on some fronts, told of the escalation of noise. The 1978 *City Planning of Tokyo* reported the expansion of the population and multi-household occupancy, and the progress of the freeway system. By 1976, 103.3 kilometers of freeway had been completed.[5] However, as Coaldrake points out, "The oil crisis of the 1970s drastically slowed the momentum of the post-war economic miracle and forced re-evaluation of existing city planning and construction."[6]

In 1971 Maki criticised the lack of concern, let alone action, on the part of the Japanese architects, claiming, "Until quite recently we, with few exceptions, have not questioned the menace of unlimited expansion of large metropolises", but "today there is increasing uneasiness and apprehension among us."[7] The hostile and polluted atmosphere of the major cities provoked a negative reaction among Japanese architects. With disillusionment over the failure of the technological dreams of the 1960s and evidence of the destruction rather than creation of the city, Japanese architects, for the most part, sought escape. They retreated from involvement with the city and, rather, attempted to provide sheltered enclaves within the madness, where their clients could hide away from the noise and smog. Buildings such as Yasuyoshi Hayashi's House with Exploded Space, 1969, aggressively accosted the city, and Takefumi Aida's Nivana Box, 1972, set blank or "dumb" walls against the urban environment. Shin Takamatsu believed that architecture had to fight to survive the Blade Runner future it faced.[8] The mechanistic imagery of his buildings confronted the city with antagonism.

The urban part

In the context of the hopelessness and frustration experienced by his colleagues, Maki's rational and realistic acceptance of the city's dilemma seems remarkable. In 1979 he wrote, "Today, our city is being forced to undergo changes which it has never experienced before. Bewildered by this kaleidoscopic world we try to cope with these changes by piecemeal treatment. Under these conditions, discovering and understanding things that do not change or are difficult to change are indeed important in order to understand what we must or can change."[9] Maki came to realise that the Metabolist vision was too ambitious and that one simply cannot change everything. In Australia he asked: "At what level can we be most effective? Then I find that architects are most useful and effective in restructuring our physical environment at a scale ranging from, say roughly, a district of several thousand inhabitants to a small neighbourhood to a complex of buildings in one block," – what he called micro-scale planning.[10] He decided that it was necessary to think small, realising that mega-interventions were beyond the architect's control. As Kuma relates: "... so then Maki tried a very sophisticated way to change the city. He was just one small point in the city. But in Japanese tradition if one person puts a small point on some areas, people can change everything."[11] In this way Maki devised a strategy in which the resolution of small parts of the city would encourage others to do the same. He resolved that in each project he would "make just one small part of the city better". This notion of "small" became central to his thinking as he realised that the smaller the project the more opportunity there was for the architect to control all parts of the design, and that to make a good city the designer had to provide many small spaces – a philosophy encapsulated in the Hillside Terraces development.

Hillside Terraces

Although Maki has been greatly influenced by the European cities and makes frequent reference to Amsterdam and Paris, he is aware of their limitations as models for the city of

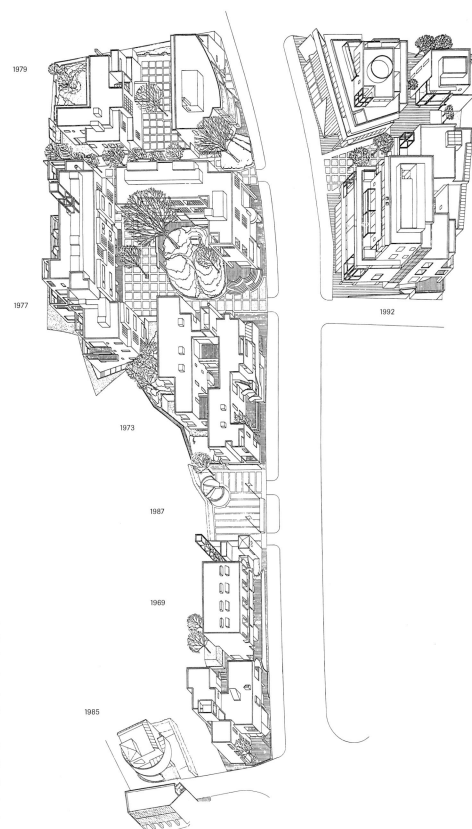

1979

1992

1977

Hillside Terraces, Tokyo. Axonometric.

1973

1987

1969

today. He has said: "The city, such as the old cities of Europe, used to dictate the form of the building, i.e. design from the outside in. Now the city does not have that power. Each building must be a city within itself. It must contain the intensity, the force, of the city."[12] Hillside Terraces is such a miniature of the city.

1985

This most engaging urban project of Maki's career (which took over twenty-five years to complete) commenced with Stage I of Hillside Terraces, a commission for the Asakura family, consisting of housing and commercial de-

velopment on a well-located site on a pleasant sloping street in the fashionable Daikanyama District of Tokyo. This is a remarkable, highly collaborative project between the family (ten members of which still live on the site) and the architect. Design and building continued in 1971 and 1975 when he received the commissions for Stage II and Stage III. Three further projects were at various stages of development

Hillside Terraces, Tokyo. Phase VI, 1992.
Courtyard.

between 1978 and 1992. The full list was Hillside Stage I, 1967–69; Hillside Stage II, 1971–73; Hillside Stage III, 1975–77; Hillside Stage IV (by Makoto Motokura who previously worked in Maki's office), 1985; Hillside Stage V, 1987; and Hillside Stage VI, 1992. Maki's Royal Danish Embassy, 1979, is built on a parcel of land that had been part of the family holding, and forms a part of the Hillside

composition. A retrospective exhibition held in Tokyo in 1992 demonstrated the remarkably complementary building up of space and form that characterises the emergence of the six stages of Hillside Terraces over such a long period. Each stage of the design grew out of, yet differed from, the previous solution, reflecting variations in building regulations, and the shifting character of the external con-

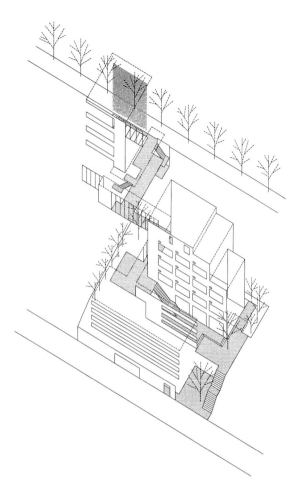

Hillside West, Tokyo, 1998. Public passage through site.

text as the street was transformed from a quiet area into a bustling and noisy thoroughfare. Since that time, some short distance along on the opposite side of the street, Maki has designed Hillside West, 1998, which continues the evolving mutations and rhythmical development of the preceding series. Important to Maki is what he has called the morphological dialogue between building and street, a theme he develops in "Street space and urban scene" published in 1974.[13] This theory underlies the total Hillside development, which consists of small "pieces", low in height, fractured in form, and generous in the provision of public space on private land. The blending of public and private has been continued into the activities, with much of the private space serving not only as meeting and gathering places but as venues for social activities such as concerts and art shows. By the time of the design of Stage VI, the ten-meter height limit along the street had been raised, but for consistency the building still aligns with the lower street profile at the front, and maximises floor space in the back section.

There is a clear evolution in the complex from the solid concrete in Stage I to the increasing lightness and use of metals in later stages, particularly in Stage VI and Hillside West. Also, the public nature of the schemes changes, becoming more open and inviting over time. Further, the stylistic bases of the units reflect Maki's aesthetic preferences and philosophical interests at the time of their design; for example, the first stage is fairly orthodox modern in its presentation, but the second stage takes a new direction. Here Maki, sympathetic to the urban nature of Venturi's "decorated shed" ideas, clearly no longer believes that the facade should reflect what is going on inside. By the third phase he is working with an independent facade. In response to the rising traffic intensity, the buildings turn away from the street and become more inward-looking, and the later projects show both an increase in the screening of the facades and, by Hillside West, the dissolving of the layers into amorphous attached skins.

Throughout Hillside Terraces the pavement is extended into the hidden or revealed pockets of public and semi-public spaces that compose the cinematic sequences of courts and corridors winding in and out of the buildings along the sloping road. Maki's analysis of the

spatial layering of the city of Tokyo, published in 1979 as his *Visible and Invisible City: A Morphological Analysis of the City of Edo-Tokyo*[14], accompanied the early designs for the Hillside Terraces, and the designs of the later stages demonstrate his findings, with more complex and penetrating public spaces within the development. Changes are evident in Stage III, with an increased cultural content in the deployment of oku, and the preservation of a sixth-century mound and shrine. By Hillside West the urban character is developed to create three blocks defining what appear as traditional streets and alleys. In the Daikanyama development Maki creates a new urbanity for the city and the times by challenging conventional thinking in terms of the deployment of land.

For all the shifts in Maki's ideas over the twenty-five years of the design of the Hillside Terraces, the general order and ambience of the work are remarkably consistent. There are degrees of change and development in each of the stages, notably in the building/street or private/public relationship, but these are subtle shifts that do not disrupt the overall accord of the composition. The designs throughout retain a restrained modernist format, without the formalism of buildings such as Iwasaki Museum, and without the vitality of the city buildings, such as Spiral, which were designed during the same period as the later three stages of Hillside Terraces. Maki has commented that the stages of Hillside Terraces are consistent despite their multiple variations, because they had one designer. But it is more than this. It is a matter of mutual respect of one building for another, the good manners that each building displays towards the street, and the application of the principles of group form and movement spaces consistently over a long period.

My Town Tokyo

In the early 1980s, Japanese cities were continuing to evolve on the pattern of constant recycling and replacement. In 1978 the total cost of new construction was about 100 billion US dollars; of this the housing, mostly wooden, represented about five percent of the cost. The cost of land in Tokyo was such that it was financially unsound to have it vacant for any period of time, and temporary building added to the transitory nature of the urban environment.

By the 1980s, the visible pollution of the cities had lessened, but although they were more aesthetically agreeable, invisible chemical pollutants remained at high contamination levels. Optimistically, the 1980 publication for the Tokyo Metropolitan Government, *Tokyo Tomorrow*,[15] introduced a new set of values into the planning of Tokyo with its theme of the "quality of life". This publication reveals the new attitudes in Japan that followed in the wake of economic recovery. These were based on both an increased awareness of the inadequacies of the public realm of the city and a desire for the "good life" that the buoyant economy could bring. The imported luxury goods in the shops, and the growing global consciousness of standards elsewhere, fostered by communications media, stimulated consumer desires. The new vision for Tokyo was voiced in *My Town Tokyo – For the Dawn of the 21st Century*, the 1991 long-term plan for the Tokyo Metropolis.[16] Japan was on its way to providing some of the richest and most dynamic settings for urban living anywhere.

The cities, at last, appeared less threatening, and were already hives of activities offering pastimes and delights of all kinds and from all over the world. The users of the cities enjoyed the delights of high technological performance and services, and the cities ap-

Tower Study for Tokyo Form and Spirit, 1985.

peared to celebrate these in tumultuous displays of flashing multi-coloured neons. Tall office blocks rose on designated sections of the cities, and industrial building and multi-level freeways multiplied along waterways and on reclaimed land, adding to the chaotic, clashing streetscape that typifies Japanese urbanity. Maki responded favourably to the evolving commercial and industrial landscape, seeing it as a logical extension of the spontaneous growth pattern that had always characterised Tokyo. Looking back over the emergence of the shifting pattern of vernacular development, he wrote in 1988, "Not only is our contemporary city composed overwhelmingly of industrial artefacts, but among these artefacts are those that have already gained an historical dimension and are becoming transmitters of messages with new meanings."[17]

Maki's acceptance of the industrial vernacular sat comfortably with the urban theories emerging in America from the writings of Venturi. Venturi and Scott Brown's advocacy of "Main Street" and "The Strip" and an acceptance of the "ordinary", notably in the 1972 publication of *Learning from Las Vegas,* called for a reassessment of conventional urban aesthetics.[18] Although the Japanese city was not

drawn on by Venturi, his writings helped widen the appreciation of differing urban constructs, including those of Japan. Venturi's theories betrayed parallels with European postmodern theories of "difference" in the following decades. Revelations in mathematics, physics and philosophy, that arose in new orders and differing interpretations of commonly accepted ways of thinking in Western culture, resulted in an enlightened re-reading of the Japanese city. This contributed to a more sympathetic perspective towards the quite different order of Tokyo. Consequently, the 1980s saw a rising general interest in the challenging, seemingly chaotic, nature of the Japanese city. In 1985 Peter Popham published his revealing interpretation, *Tokyo: City at the End of the World,*[19] and in 1989 Ashihara provided the Japanese perspective on the city in the English publication of his book, *Hidden Orders/Tokyo Through the Twentieth Century.*[20] This was followed considerably later, in 1999, by Barrie Shelton's appreciative book *Learning from the Japanese City: West Meets East in Urban Design.*[21] In Popham's and Sheldon's books, the readings of Tokyo are from a Western perspective, so over the last two decades of the twentieth century an attempt was being

Tokyo Metropolitan Gymnasium: Cloud image.

made, both from within Japan and without, not to condemn Japanese cities, but to reassess such urban giants on their own terms.

Maki and the urban metaphor

The urban constructs of Maki's architecture up to the 1980s involved exploratory concepts for remedial interventions in urban form. But with an awareness of the futility, or even undesirability, of confronting the tide of urban development, his more recent projects are intended to be reflective rather than curative, presenting an architecture that "is at once an embodiment and a reflection of the city".[22] For, although Maki's new architecture is anti-utopian, it suggests an awareness of the possibilities of accepting and engaging the given urban situation: "We must now see our urban society as a dynamic field of interrelated forces. It is a set of mutually independent variables in a rapidly expanding infinite series. Any order introduced within the pattern of forces contributes to the state of dynamic equilibrium."[23] Maki seeks to interpret and communicate existence in the city, and the city

becomes a manifestation of contemporary experience, with architecture its mimetic representation. Tokyo emerged from a life-view and historical circumstances that gave rise to a restless city of randomness and impermanence, and, as it provides clear evidence of the effects of advancing technology and the consequent systems of dispersion and change, so it serves well as a metaphor and operative model for contemporary life. Further, it mirrors today's world through the lack of static or constant definition, and the absence of structured form in the city prevents any grasp of its totality, let alone any portrayal of that totality. Maki draws on such urban metaphors in pursuit of meaningful interpretations of the nature of postmodern phenomena. In his architecture the city, notably Tokyo, figures as a symbolic bridge between the seen state of existence today and the building as an embodiment of that condition.

Maki's vision of Tokyo is clearly grounded in history. He sees in the impermanence of Japanese cities a state of undifferentiation, appropriately attuned to current conscious-

ness. For Maki the city bears witness to this reality, and provides a link between the inconceivable and the partially conceivable. The 1985 Exhibition "Tokyo Form and Spirit", displayed first in Japan and then in the United States, provided the opportunity to project his thinking on major urban works at a conceptual level. Maki's installation represented a collection of six column "trees" designed in conjunction with the sculptor Kiyoshi Awazu. The "trees" making up the "forest" of the city denoted certain characteristics of Tokyo: Metropolitan Life machine, The Caterpillar City, The Headquarters, Yagura (fire-tower) Festival, Life and Death of Great Japanese City, and Oku.[24] This was accompanied by a volume of essays bearing the same title, produced in a well-illustrated volume edited by Mildred Friedman.[25] At a more literal level, as with Spiral, also 1985, the city's elements and morphology are drawn on to produce buildings that "look to some extent like chaotic Tokyo".[26] The identifiable characteristics of the city are represented by Maki's imagery of the "fragment" and the "cloud".[27]

Tepia, Tokyo, 1989. Filtering screens.

The fragment and the cloud

The designs for the Hillside Terraces Stages IV, V and VI were paralleled by further explorations of the urban structure of Tokyo, leading to Maki's theories on the fractured nature of the city. This gave rise to two strategies to work with in the city – the "fragment" and the "cloud". His principal buildings of the following years can be seen to belong to one or other of these strategic families.[28] These groupings, as far as relations with the city are concerned, sit reasonably comfortably with Maki's patterns of spatial constructs of this same period; that is, the "fragment" buildings are mostly spatially linear in organisation and establish particular connections with the city, while the "cloud" buildings consist of grouped parts which are tightly related among themselves. The "fractured" buildings can be seen as members of his classic building tradition, yet eroded by the forces of the city. The cloud buildings are represented by the great hovering roof volumes of the wide-span structures.

The urban context for these late buildings was one of increasing dynamism and fluctuating change. In the 1980s the constraints on industry, and consequently on the economy, caused by the oil crisis had passed and Japan began on the upward spiral of an economic boom that resulted in the "bubble" economy of the end of the decade.

Fragment

Maki views the city primarily as a physical entity. For him, the constant change and regeneration of the consumer city denies the viability of any notions of closed and complete compositions relating part to whole. Clearly evident in Maki's work of the 1980s and 1990s, but especially in Spiral, Tepia, and the YKK Research Center, are loosely structured geometric ideas that are open to shifts and elaborations. The buildings are but fracturing elements in the fracturing city. In his recent interpretations, the part appears as the fragment, substituting for that which is unimaginable in its totality, and arousing fleeting sensations of recognition. Maki's current architecture derives to a marked extent from the various uses of that which is only partially comprehensible to project a simulation of the structure of the city, and of the drives and directives that have given it form.

Maki first used the term "fragment" in 1974 when he said that the "city has been intensely fragmented"[29] and Spiral provides a fragmenting miniature of the city in the midst of

Spiral, Tokyo, 1985.

its dizzy prosperity. Spiral's facade holds up a mirror to the city – a mirror that captures the image of the bits and pieces of the urban landscape and magically turns them into a major art form as if through a kaleidoscope. The bits are still there and belong with the city but have passed through some distinctive transformation. The building takes its place cheek-by-jowl with the other commercial buildings on Aoyama Dori and in its mass, it vanishes as a fragment of the city block. Spatially, Spiral extends the by-ways and side-ways of the city with twisting "oku" concealing paths and the temptations of what lies unexplored ahead.

Spiral was followed by further city buildings that developed particular relationships with the city. The nearby Tepia establishes a haunting, veiled connection to the city, whereby the city, in a muted and shadowy way, is made evident through walls of filtering screens, and glimpses of partial views are revealed through slivers of overlapping or angled planes.

Cloud

In his second reading of Tokyo, Maki identifies the characteristics of the city as lightness, impermanence, complexity, heterogeneity and flux. It is in this sense that he uses a cloud analogy to convey unsubstantiality and indefinability. This reading is represented by a series of dramatic, large-span buildings, including Fujisawa Gymnasium, 1984, Makuhari Messe, Tokyo Bay, 1989, and the Tokyo Metropolitan Gymnasium, 1990. For Maki the "cloud" buildings represent a different urban order. They are not active participants in the city, neither do they reflect its patterns. Rather, they typically gather in a clearly defined enclave, and are commonly set apart from their surroundings by a podium. In these buildings the sensuous, curving roof forms, sheathed with gleaming metallic skins, seem to vibrate and drift over the cavernous spaces of the halls. Yet Maki's architecture exhibits no tendency to dematerialisation except through light. These buildings are essentially tectonic in expression – experiential entities that insist on their own presence and textuality.

1990s and onwards – The tower

In the 1990s Maki became interested in the tower form as an urban element. In 1994 he designed the Bayside Tower, Yokohama. This hybrid project is made up of a relocated original facade of a 1930s building, the reproduction of the rest of the early building, and a new

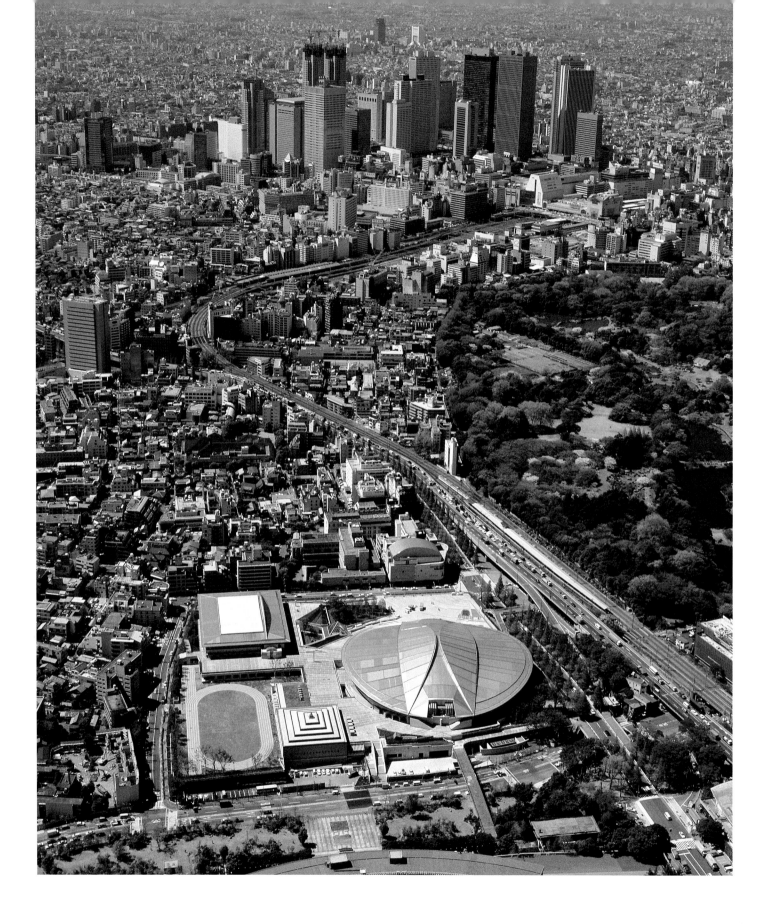

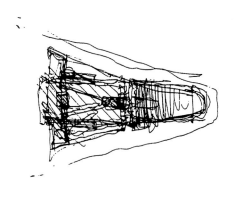

Yokohama Bayside Tower, Yokohama, 2003. Sketch of plan.

Yokohama Bayside Tower, Yokohama, 2003. Conceptual sketch.

Tokyo Metropolitan Gymnasium, Tokyo, 1990.

tower with an aluminium and glass curtain wall. These disparate parts are congenially combined by Maki's overall scheme in which the tower extends the form and order of the old building, and presents a contrasting face on the opposite facade. The project is due for completion in 2003. But Maki's most resolved and elegant tower was designed in 1999 as a competition project for residential and office accommodation in the town of Vuosaari outside Helsinki. There is a consonance in this design from the detail of the individual units to the seemingly inevitable "fit" with the town plan. The tower plan consists of two splayed-apart parallelograms cased in glass, with a joining service core forming a void that serves as an exhaust duct. The angular shape slots neatly into the town plan, allows maximum views of the sea, and is functionally and struc-

turally efficient. Although unbuilt, this fractured urban gesture in minimalist dress is one of Maki's most resolved urban proposals.

Maki's studies of the 1970s increased his understanding of urbanism, and his writings and buildings through the 1980s and 1990s reveal the continuity of his deep preoccupation with the city. In particular, Tokyo constantly serves as the focus for his urban theories, and his interventions always engage with and contribute to the urban fabric. Over the last three decades of the twentieth century, the Japanese city passed from decline to resurrection, but Maki never turned his back on the Japanese city, nor lost faith in its offerings. In addition, in the 1990s he entered into dialogue with the American and European city.[30]

Yokohama Bayside Tower, Yokohama, 2003.

Vuosaari Tower, Vuosaari, Finland, 1999. Perspective drawing.

Yerba Buena Gardens Visual Arts Center, San Francisco, 1993.

Vuosaari Tower, Vuosaari, Finland, 1999. Compositional plan.

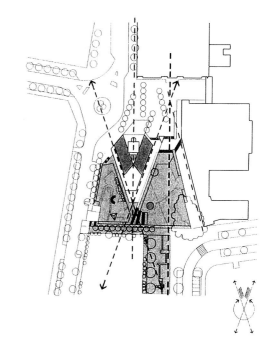

Notes

1 Fumihiko Maki, "The potential of planning", *Architecture in Australia,* 60 (4), August 1971, p. 695.

2 Maki, "The potential of planning", p. 700.

3 Shunichi Watanabe and Satoshi Morito, "Megalopolis in Japan: urbanism as a way of business", *Ekistics,* 226, 1974, pp. 161–62, and Catharine Nagashima, "Some definitions of megalopolis in Japan", *Ekistics,* 226, 1974, pp. 163–69. Both of these papers were delivered at the Seminar on the International Comparative Study on Megalopolises held in Tokyo in June 1973.

4 For example, *Tokyo Fights Pollution: An Urgent Appeal for Reform,* Tokyo, Tokyo Metropolitan Government, 1971; *City Planning of Tokyo,* Tokyo Municipal Government, 1978.

5 *City Planning of Tokyo,* p. 114.

6 William H. Coaldrake, "Order and anarchy: Tokyo from 1868 to the present", in Mildred Friedman (ed.), *Tokyo: Form and Spirit,* Minneapolis, Walker Art Center and New York, Harry N. Abrams Inc., 1986, p. 63.

7 Maki, "The potential of planning", p. 696.

8 Conversation with Shin Takamatsu, Kyoto, 1986.

9 Fumihiko Maki, "Japanese city spaces and the concept of "oku'", *The Japan Architect,* 54, 5 (265), 1979, p. 52.

10 Maki, "The potential of planning", p. 696.

11 Conversation with Kenzo Kuma, Tokyo, 1995.

12 Conversation with Maki, Tokyo, 1995.

13 Fumihiko Maki, "Street space and the urban scene", *The Japan Architect,* 49, 1 (205), 1974, pp. 42–44.

14 Fumihiko Maki, *Visible and Invisible City: A Morphological Analysis of the City of Edo-Tokyo,* Tokyo, Kajima Publishing Co., 1979.

15 "Tokyo Tomorrow", Tokyo Municipal Library No. 17, 1980.

16 The 3rd Long-Term Plan for the Tokyo Metropolis (Outline), "My Town Tokyo" – For the Dawn of the 21st Century, Tokyo, Tokyo Municipal Library No. 25, 1991.

17 Fumihiko Maki, "Toward an industrial vernacular" (manuscript), published as "City image, materiality" in Serge Salat and Françoise Labbé (eds.), *Fumihiko Maki: An Aesthetic of Fragmentation,* New York, Rizzoli, 1988, p. 7 (previously published in French by Electa-Moniteur).

18 Robert Venturi, Denise Scott Brown, Steven Inezour, *Learning from Las Vegas,* Cambridge, Mass., MIT Press, 1972. However, in 1975 Maki had asked, "But must we resort to the kind of solution symbolised by Las Vegas?"

19 Peter Popham, *Tokyo: The City at the End of the World,* Tokyo, Kodansha International, 1985.

20 Yoshinobu Ashihara, *Hidden Orders/Tokyo Through the Twentieth Century,* Tokyo/New York, Kodansha International, 1989.

21 Barrie Shelton, *Learning from the Japanese City: West Meets East in Urban Design,* London, E & FN Spon, 1999.

22 Fumihiko Maki, "Driving force of the 1990s", *The Japan Architect,* Annual, Spring, 2, 1991, p. 11.

23 Fumihiko Maki, "Space, image and materiality", *The Japan Architect,* 16, Special Issue on Fumihiko Maki, Winter 4, 1994 pp. 4–13.

24 "Tokyo Form and Spirit Exhibition", 1985, organised by the Walker Art Center, Minneapolis, in association with the Japan House Gallery. The exhibition was on tour in the United States 1986–87 and showed the projects of seven teams.

25 Mildred Friedman (ed.), *Tokyo: Form and Spirit,* Minneapolis, Walker Art Center, and New York, Harry N. Abrams Inc., 1986.

26 Maki, quoted in *An Aesthetic of Fragmentation,* p. 29.

27 Serge Salat discusses this in *An Aesthetic of Fragmentation,* pp. 19–33.

28 This aspect of Maki's work also has been well discussed in Salat's text.

29 Maki, "Street space and the urban scene", p. 42.

30 His engagement in the United States came through the design for the Yerba Buena Gardens Visual Arts Center in San Francisco. This museum is one of several buildings for the redevelopment complex south of Market Street in downtown San Francisco, which, due to the politics of the development, had a very long construction history.

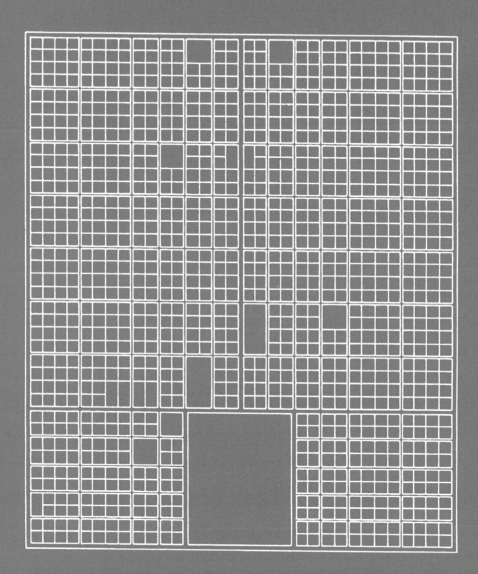

Early Kyoto city plan.

8 Order: Reading of Order and Image

The prosperity of Japan continued to increase in the 1970s and, by the end of the decade, Japanese architecture started to show signs of idiosyncratic indulgence-stemming, in part, from affluence. The publication of Robert Venturi's *Complexity and Contradiction in Architecture* in 1966 had pointed the way to a loosening of orthodox modernist dogmas, allowing a freer rein for individual expression. By the early 1970s Venturi's theories had reached a sympathetic audience in America and elsewhere, but the influence of popularist postmodern architecture that followed in the wake had little impact in Japan until the end of the decade. Japan in the 1970s was concerned with re-establishing social and political order and cultural prestige. In architecture, this was represented by new government, community and art buildings. These were usually imposing works, often using rich materials, and dominating the small-scale vernacular fabric of the towns. They served primarily as emblems of status, proclaiming the worthiness of the particular communities. However, with the exception of a major under-taking for the National Museum of Art, Kyoto, Maki's commissions of the 1970s tended to be from private rather than government sources, following on from those with which he had commenced his practice in the 1960s.

In Maki's writings and buildings of the late 1970s and 1980s, there is a fresh exploration of the notion of complexity as a real and involving attribute of the time, and an increased interest in the possibilities of symbolic representation in architecture. Both of these explorations were deployed by Maki to extend the constricting limitations of the dogmas of the Modern Movement. That is, he sought a rejuvenation of a tired modernism, and its transformation into a rich and revealing architecture appropriate to the late twentieth century. In these regards Maki acknowledges his debt to some fellow architects: "Statements of belief by certain architects made a particularly strong impression on me. One was *Complexity and Contradiction in Architecture* (1966) by Robert Venturi. I was also stirred by the espousal of an 'inclusive architecture' by architects such as Charles Moore and Robert Stern. They denied the existence of absolute criteria, cast doubt on the inevitability of progress, and regarded compositional principles as subject to external forces but ultimately based on architecture's own rules."[1] Maki states, "I identify with the School of Complexity."[2] He specifically comments positively on the thinking encapsulated in Venturi's "difficult whole". Accord is expressed by Venturi who, in writing on the "difficult whole", refers to Maki's work: "The very complex building, which in its open form is incomplete, in itself relates to Maki's 'group form'; it is the antithesis of the 'perfect single building' or the closed pavilion."[3]

Although some of these influences surface in the bold colours and supergraphics that occasionally appear in his schools of the 1970s, Maki's architecture bears little resemblance to the popularist indulgences and excesses of American postmodern architecture. In a formal sense, Maki's buildings of the 1970s have more in common with the early white architecture of Le Corbusier and hence share superficial similarities with the

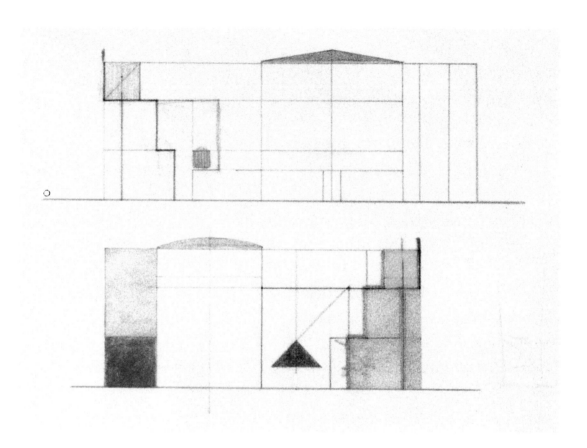

Tepia, Tokyo, 1989. Concept drawing.

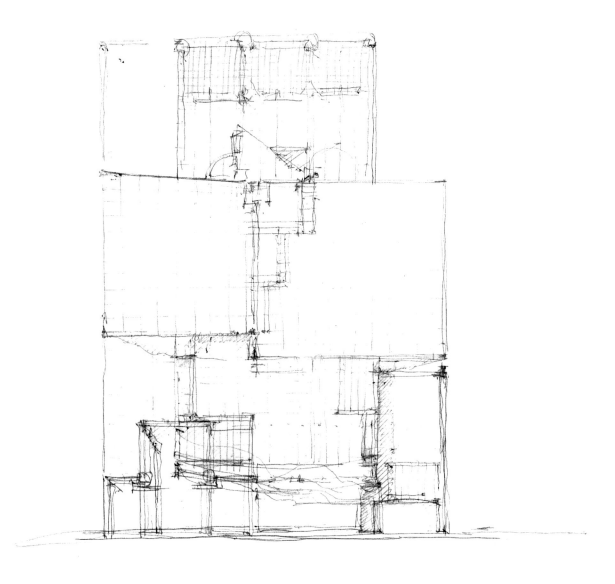

Spiral, Tokyo, 1985. Early sketch.

National Museum of Modern Art, Kyoto, 1986. Facade study.

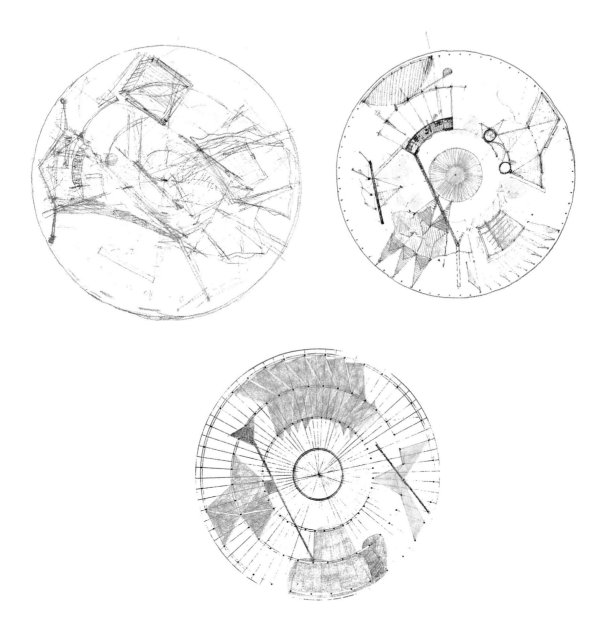

Zeebrugge Ferry Terminal, Holland, 1989. Conceptual constellation.

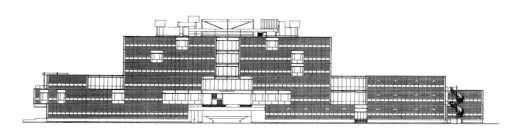

Tsukuba University Central Building for Physical Education
and Art, Ibaraki, 1974.
South elevation.

Amboise, April 4, 1981. Sketch by Maki.

1970s work of the New York Five, such as that by Richard Meier. In his hands, theoretical ideas were translated through the Japanese perspective, and the buildings emerged with a customary elegance and restraint. This is supported by Suzuki, who claims that Maki has the ability to approach design in many different ways, but no matter what method he uses he refines it and makes it his own.[4]

Maki's work is neither historically retrogressive nor does it offer a social and architectural critique of the American architects. Rather, Maki flirts with the signature pieces of modern architecture, such as Casa del Fascio and Villa Savoye, but transforms them in their rearrangement and, at Keio University Shonan Fujisawa Campus, by multiplicity. Kuma describes Maki's use of Western references as a kind of sophisticated game that he is always playing. "He does not like literal quotations, but enjoys the situation when some can find original form in his work, but others cannot."[5] For "without ever contradicting the modern tenets of truth to materials, and form follows function, Maki recognises other romantic,

symbolic and monumental layers to his architectural creations. There is also a deliberate playfulness in his work."[6] Although his revision of modern architecture did involve the erosion of its rigid and unbending logic of rationalist order, he remained within the arms of the modern, retaining its ambitions but widening its embrace and enriching its language. Maki explains his continuing relationship with modernism, seeing its continuing relevance because "it is in fact a system of change".[7] As Hiroyuki Suzuki states, "Modernity is a condition of our society. So he [Maki] stands on the condition of modernity and expresses himself using every architecture of modern society because he is a product of modernity. ... His architecture is always his."[8] Stewart also expresses this well as "... uncompromisingly Western and indeed international in style. In essence and detailing it is Japanese, but within the limits of Maki's own resolutely contemporary idiom."[9]

Remaining fundamental to Maki's architecture of the 1970s and 1980s is the desire to make an architecture that is both compre-

hensible in its message and evident in its genesis. The representation embedded in the work, and the harnessing of the complex nature of its program and place, are given expression through the order and imagery of the composition. The ultimate aim is the creation of an architecture that can communicate "unconscious group aspiration" which, writing in 1999, Maki states has been "the most important fruit of my work in recent years".[10]

Highly revealing of Maki's compositional principles is *Fragmentary Figures: The Collected Architectural Drawings*, a book of sketches he published in 1989.[11] The fine, mostly small, sketches contained in the book include vignettes of architecture that caught his eye on his travels. Yet the main body of the collection consists of Maki's design sketches, through which it is possible to trace the emergence of the building from the idea to the form through his manipulation of lines, planes and points. For Maki, the sketch is particularly personal and revealing: "Sketches mirror the 'self' and at the same time clearly reveal the

Tepia, Tokyo, 1989.

tastes and limitations of the architect. An architect's predilection for certain forms defines the scope of his imagination."[12]

Classic Maki

With the buildings of the late 1970s and early 1980s Maki introduced a new mode of composition to his repertoire that might well be called "Classic Maki". Significant works of this ilk are Maki's house, Tokyo, 1978, the National Museum of Modern Art, Kyoto, commenced in 1978 and completed in 1986, the Iwasaki Art Museum, Ibuski, 1979 (annex 1987), the New Library for the Mita Campus of Keio University, 1981, and the YKK Guest House, Kurobe, 1982. The later Spiral, 1985,

and Tepia, 1989, in Tokyo, clearly belong to this family, as do the regimented blocks of the Keio University Shonan Fujisawa Campus, 1994. At least to begin with, Maki's approach in this complex is well-mannered and disciplined, perhaps in order to counter the vulgarity of much contemporary architecture. The internal rhythms and patterns of the spatial composition are contained by precise planar facades, designed with the geometric balance of De Stijl. Clearly, the Schroeder House (which Maki had visited with van Eyck in the late 1960s) provided direct inspiration for such compositions, as in the design of Tepia. This is a cool, geometric architecture with the clarity and control one might associate with

Louis Kahn's best buildings. This is not surprising as Maki was an admirer of Kahn who served as a reference point for his work in the 1960s. In this phase in Maki's career seemingly concise and balanced forms are restrained to the point of apparent serenity. Closer scrutiny of the work, notably the later buildings, however, reveals a willful and challenging divergence within the overall restraint.

With their complex yet clarified interiors and floating facade planes, the buildings of the 1960s such as the Toyoda Memorial Hall and the Senri Civic Center testify as the archaic precursors to the more classic works of the 1970s and 1980s. Similarly, the regular order of the planar facades of the National Aquari-

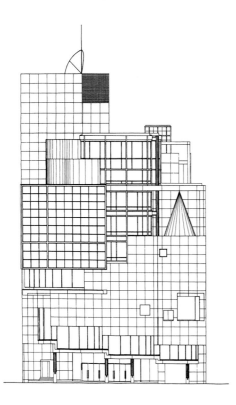

Spiral, Tokyo, 1985. Elevation.

Maki House, Tokyo, 1978. Front facade.

um, Okinawa, 1975, and the Tsukuba University Central Building, 1976, presents a certain frontality that characterises the works that came later. The powerful facade of the Tsukuba building, which forms a portal on a principal axial campus crossing, clearly is a precursor to the commanding, balanced facade of the National Museum in Kyoto.

But the "classic" buildings of the 1970s and 1980s, although initially appearing stable and resolved, evidence hidden sets of contrary compositional relationships, such as emerge in the erosion of Spiral and the dissection of Tepia. For example, the pattern of development in these studies evolved from the stable forms of Maki's house to a mannerist transformation of the same basic form in the eclectic facade of Spiral. Related manneristic traits are evident in the way the clarity of the containing and space-defining planes in Maki's residence are blurred to become the indistinct spatial layering of Tepia. Despite the subver-

sive undermining of the rigid discipline of order, Maki's architecture retains an aloof and precise presence, encapsulating a different permissive order and revealing its subtleties primarily through the experience of the architecture.

So, although superficially this appears as a Euclidean architecture, further study of the buildings reveals a subversive shifting within the diagrammatic order, maintaining its reassuring sense of stability while providing diverting and engaging spatial and temporal events. For within the satisfying appearance of resolution and stability, these buildings house displacement and tension, which eventually crack open the shell of the orderly geometry in the roof forms of the YKK Research Center, and finally break free in the torsional podium and roof of the Kirishima Concert Hall. The subtle deviations, sequences and nuances found in Maki's "classic" work are also evidenced in traditional

design such as that of the garden and buildings of the seventeenth-century Katsura Detached Palace in Kyoto. However, as Suzuki points out, "He quite consciously destroys the strict application of the modern principles and he does not use strict traditional compositions. He doesn't use either this principle or that principle. He finds his own place in-between the order."[13]

Today in world architecture there is a searching for new forms of order beyond the constraints of those imposed by Western doctrine, in order to denote a certain security within the dynamic of the times. Maki's displaced and blurred Classicism in these geometrically founded buildings throws further into relief the complementary and opposing thrusts in his work of a rationalistic logic and an intuitive relaxed creativity. One provides control, the other liberty.

YKK Research Center, Tokyo, 1993.

Order and imagery

The conception of these "classic" buildings is based on Maki's belief that it is the task of the architect "no matter what the era, to elicit from complex phenomena, and give expression to primary symbolism ... ",[14] and that it is the architect's task to seek the inherent order in the complexity, and provide a fundamental, readable, symbolic code in the archi-

tecture. This duality is realized in the "classic" buildings through the marriage of Palladian and Japanese constructs, combining Western classical modes of composition, including the Platonic solids (and their deployment in modern architecture), with the layered space and all-pervading lineal discipline of Japanese traditional design. The resulting architecture has the poise and appar-

New Library, Keio University, Mita Campus, Tokyo, 1981.

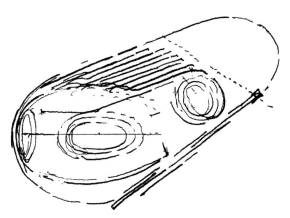

Queensland Gallery of Modern Art, Brisbane, Australia, 2001. Conceptual plan.

ent resolution of the European villa, yet it is imbued with unanticipated and seductive depths.

Order

Maki's classic buildings have an all-pervading sense of resolution arising from an overall geometric order. He has frequently remarked that the role of architecture is "always the integration and formation of order".[15] This order is delineated in the building by the horizontal and vertical planes, the lines and the points. It is basically a geometric construct and rarely does one find organic free-forms in his work before the 1990s. In writing on Tepia, Maki comments that "the overall architectural aesthetic is ruled by a compositional principle based throughout on planes and straight lines."[16] This order is not the result of a rigid application of rules; rather it is permissive and

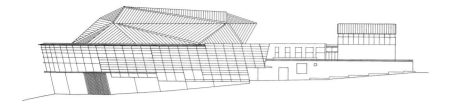

Kirishima International Concert Hall,
Kagoshima, 1994. North elevation.

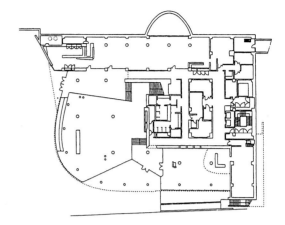

Fukuoka University, Helios Plaza, 1996.
First floor plan.

accommodating and, as in the past, acts as "the agent that effects physical and spiritual coherence in building" and as the spiritual principle in "the subjection of building to a major ethical concept".[17] This De Stijl adherence to orthogonal geometry gives way in later work to allow arching roof forms, as at the Fujisawa Gymnasium, and curving walls, as with the Keio University Graduate Research Center at the Shonan Campus. By the 1990s Maki's work had become far more inclusive in its use of forms, with irregular shapes and curves commonly dominating the composition, such as at the Kirishima Concert Hall, 1994, the Graduate Research School at Keio University, 1994, Fukuoka University Helios Plaza, 1996, Kanagawa University Auditorium, 1996, and the Asahi Broadcasting Center in Roppongi, Tokyo, due for completion in 2003. A further example of these curved forms appears in the competition entry for the Queensland Gallery of Modern Art, Brisbane, 2001. Here the curved surfaces intersect with angular penetrations, contrasting with the rectangular forms of the buildings in the immediate area. Maki's late interest in curved forms is evidenced again in one of his most sensuous works – the machine laboratory of the Triad, Hotaka, Nagano, 2002, which is cased in a singular, slinky, distorted tubular form of gleaming metal.

Modular proportion

Historically, Japanese architecture has been based on a modular system determined by the *tatami* method or the post method of measurement and building layout. The structural order then determines the spatial order. As Carver points out, "The clue to these spatial mechanics is structure which acts as the coordinates of a spatial organisation outlining by implication and suggestion its essential geometrical order."[18] In the eyes of the early European modernists, such as Taut and Gropius, the accord evident between these methods of organisation and the modular dictates of the machine established a clear affinity between Japanese building customs and modern architecture. Hence, in this regard, Maki's architecture shows no discord between the two traditions. To the basic structural modular organization Maki adds the tripartite subdivisions of the Western classical world. This use of the tripartite organisation of the masses in the vertical dimension is evident in most of the buildings of this time, many of which stand on plinths and terminate in various manners substituting for the traditional cornice. These range from the stepping down of the building's silhouette, as at the Tsukuba Central Building and the New Keio University Library, to the penthouse of Spiral and the tense horizontal roof plane of Tepia.

Grid

The grid in traditional Japanese architecture is generally determined by the proportions of the structural module. The geometry is integral to the design and is made evident primarily in the patterns of squares and rectangles contained in the modular dimensions of the structure and section. Related rectangular geometries provide sub- and sub-sub-levels of patterning that permeate the entire building. The dominant visual characteristic of much Japan-

Spiral, Tokyo, 1985. Facade *shoji* detail.

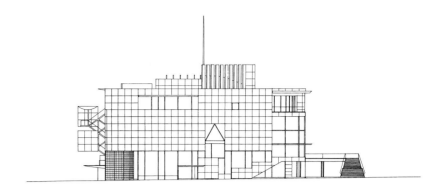

Tepia, Tokyo, 1989. Elevations.

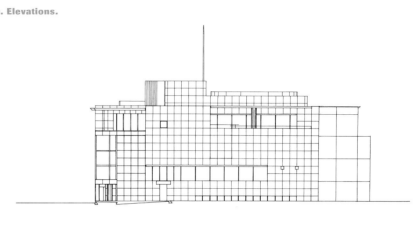

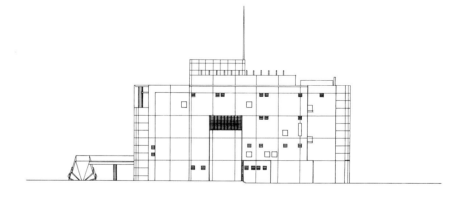

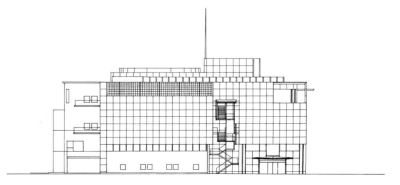

ese traditional architecture is the covering of surfaces with an all-pervading pattern of rectangles and squares of all sizes.

The grid has served as a favoured compositional device in contemporary architecture. Surface as gridded patterns appeared in the 1970s in the designs of architects such as Richard Meier in America and Isozaki and Maki in Japan, and in Kahn's highly influential Center for British Art and Studies, Yale University, of 1974. In these buildings the explicit patterning comes from the use of modular pre-finished cladding materials such as ceramic tiles and metal panels. Such an enveloping grid remains one of the hallmarks of Japanese architecture today, but, as Watanabe states, "With Maki the grid is one icon out of many. It is one symbol to be incorporated, not necessarily the basis of the work. For him it is sort of sacred."[19]

Generally, the grid is subservient in Maki's early period but visually dominates as an ordering, technical and decorative device from the late 1970s onward. It appears on the interior and exterior of the building, in fixtures such as doors and screens, and in fittings such as lampshades. Of interest are Maki's conceptual sketches that demonstrate how the de-

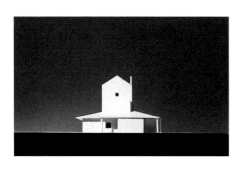

Cracow Children's Home, Poland, 1990.
Model, south and north elevations.

Toyama Shimin Plaza, 1989, Toyama.

signs commonly emerge from a two-dimensional grid – the early drawings for Spiral provide remarkable examples.[20] Among the early projects that derive their aesthetic from the dominance of various grid systems is the Tsukuba University Central Building, 1976, where the major and minor rhythms of the structural frame and the glass-block panels give the building a memorable image and sense of solidarity, even majesty. The New Library for Keio University, Mita Campus, achieves a similar stature, in this case through the use of salmon-coloured, chequered tiles that cover its surfaces and reinforce the module and overall geometry of the building's composition. The YKK Research Center boasts a remarkable entrance atrium in the form of a gridded box that appears to be clipped on to the walls of the major edifice. In the glass wall of the swimming pool of the Tokyo Metropoli-

tan Gymnasium, the grid appears as mullions, and overhead in the teflon roof as slatted latticework.[21] In many works, as in the Toyama International Conference Center, 1999, the squared wooden grill serves as a screening device, and so on.

In Maki's work, the grid is not an anonymous distancing device as one finds it in Bernard Tschumi's designs, or a negating and numbing envelope as in Fujii Hiromi's work; rather it appears as an compositional foundation for design. The grid is exploited in Maki's architecture for its underlying order, but also for the decorative aspect of the pattern it gives and the rhythms it establishes. Also of importance is the uniformity of the grid, the absence of a focusing center and its fundamental abstraction. It guides and indicates proportion, and both negates and offers readings of scale. Perhaps of even greater significance are the

symbolic qualities of its universality, the denotation of human design rather than natural occurrence. The practice of working with the grid has been reinforced in Maki's designs since he commenced drawing in a gridded sketchbook for his preliminary exploratory design sketches; the ruled sheets, Maki claims, were chosen for dimensioning.[22]

The grid is used by Maki primarily as an abstract controlling geometry, and in all of these buildings there is a clear order induced by its discipline. In the YKK Guest House, however, the grid not only serves as the mode of ordering the building but takes on a decorative quality with light honey-coloured timbers and translucent glass. At Spiral it also assumes a symbolic role in the large angled panel of the facade that clearly refers to the *shoji* screen. Further, at Spiral the grid takes on an imagery, providing shifts between order

Salzburg Congress Centre, Austria, 1992. East facade.

and disorder reflecting the patterning of the city. It is in Tepia that Maki exploits the beauty of the gridded patterns in their most refined form. The grid, once again, provides the order and rhythm throughout. Its elegance is everywhere. Of particular note is the refinement of the facades where glass sheets and fine aluminium panels are aligned in harmonious juxtaposition.

Primary forms

Maki's predilection for the purity of simple geometric figures and primary forms is explicit in the "classic" buildings. Squares, triangles and rectangles, together with cones, pyramids and cubes, provide a universally recognisable language. The purity of the primary forms endows the work with a sense of eternal order and stability. Yet, while the elements themselves are conventional, Maki's handling and placement of them is not. Such forms provide a further link between Maki and the Western classical tradition, and more immediately with modern architecture, notably the use of the primary geometric forms by Le Corbusier. In Maki's architecture the square and its derivatives are the most pervading figures; it appears repeatedly in plan and section and on

Toyama Shimin Plaza, 1989, Toyama.

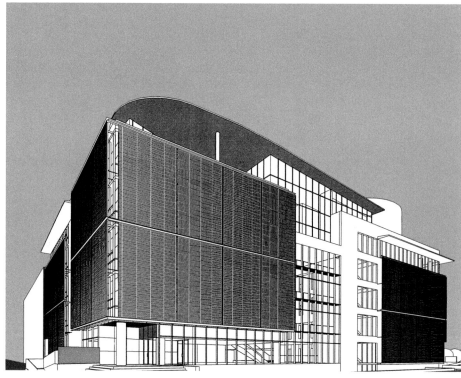

MIT Media Laboratory, Boston, 2005.
Perspective drawing.

surfaces. For example, in the unbuilt project for the Cracow Children's Home, Poland, 1990, the plan is a square and the volumes are two cubes stacked on each other. Many of Maki's buildings emerge in the early design stages as single units cut from the mesh of gridded quadrilateral blocks or those of other basic primary forms. The preliminary sketches for the Kyoto Museum and the Dentsu Advertising Building show the development of the shape of the building masses out of such a simple volumetric framework, in much the same way as facades are generated from planar grids. Such an emanation from a simple lined volume remains evident at Tepia, where Maki first drew a cubic glass box delineated in such a way as to imply that the building would be

composed of layers of planes in each direction. Design work started with Maki's image sketch of a cubic glass pavilion. It implicitly suggested how the whole building would be conceptually composed of layers of horizontal and vertical planes.

The most powerful of Maki's geometric masses is the solemn rectangular grey granite block of the Kyoto Museum. Of further interest is Maki's use of the triangle and cone which appear to be endowed with some ritualistic significance. The triangle appears as a major motif on building facades, such as at Toyama Shimin Plaza, as a central voided pediment on the main facade, and on the side walls of the National Museum of Modern Art, where it is also accorded special status as the decorative motif in the

central stairwell. But the most arresting triangular image is in the iconic cone on the facade of Spiral, which provides an arresting counterpoint to the rectangular organisation of the rest of the building. In 1990 Maki extended his exploration of compositions with geometric absolutes at the Tokyo Gymnasium where the roofs of the various stadia, sunken below the plaza, protrude as a collection of geometrically shaped tumuli on a moonscape plateau, producing a large-scale abstract garden.

The Salzburg Congress Center competition, 1992, represents Maki's purist architectural statement in presenting a Platonic cubic volume. The skin of the cube consists of finely layered transparent and translucent sheets of glass, and perforated aluminium louvres,

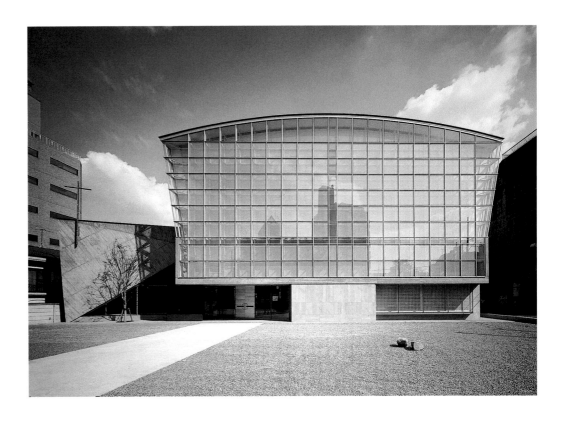

Tokyo Church of Christ, Tokyo, 1995.

shimmering by day and glowing by night.[23] The major interior volumes are held free as objects floating in space, bringing to mind Tatlin's Monument to the Third International, 1920. The cubic volume also has affinities with Rem Koolhaas's entry for the National Library, Paris, 1989, and Toyo Ito's Mediatheque designed in the mid-1990s.

Planes

The significance of the play with planes further suggest a connection between Maki's formal concerns and the earlier studies in compositions of planes in Cubism and De Stijl. Also, Maki's studies of the spatial construct of Tokyo revealed the creation of depth and a sense of *oku* by layered screening in the long narrow lots of the flat lands. So the spatial pos-sibilities of the arrangement of planes rein-troduce Japanese notions of layering and depth. Further, as in the Toyama Shimin Plaza, 1989, and the YKK Research Center, 1982, Maki cuts openings into walls to provide tan-talising glimpses of that which is beyond or promises of unseen realms yet to be reached. Explorations in layering with multiple planes are evident in Maki's work, as at the YKK Guest House and the Toyama Shimin Plaza, and also in layering within a single plane, as in the multi-shrouded walls of Tepia, where magical walls of diaphanous or translucent or perforated layered skins seduce by partly revealing what is beyond. Ethereal is the vast layered glass wall of the Tokyo Church of Christ, 1995, which forms the sanctuary wall behind the altar and separates the interior meditative space from the noisy street outside. This remarkable wall consists of two skins, the double glass-layered outer skin coated with an exterior ceramic frit to reduce heat gain and glare from the western exposure, and an inner skin of double-layered lightly sandblasted glass with two thin sheets of fibreglass between to give a milky *shoji*-like glow. A Vierendeel truss separates and supports the skins, and the space created reduces sound and increases insulation and acts as a return plenum duct for the ventilation system.

Various kinds of screening are constantly explored in search of further visual, spatial and lighting effects. Heavy timber-gridded screens order the Toyama International Con-ference Center, wide vertical perforated alu-minium blades protect the Keio University

Toyama International Conference Center, Toyama, 1999.
Timber screens.

Asahi Broadcast Center, Minato-ku, Tokyo, 2003.

YKK Research Center, Tokyo, 1993.

Graduate Research Center, and a louvre screen of fine horizontal aluminium pipes sheathes the street facade of Hillside West. In the Asahi Broadcasting Center an irregular curving skin of eaves and louvres follows the site outline, enfolding the regular orthogonal building inside. This notion of the building in a cage picks up from the Salzburg Congress Center project. Maki's use of layered planes, however, remains subtle and does not reach the point of being an evident exercise in exploring the extremes of the phenomenon, as in the work of other Japanese architects, notably Takefumi Aida. The planes are important compositional elements to Maki in the way they are used to establish lines of tension in the building. This becomes particularly clear in later works such as Spiral and Tepia, where the separating and angling of the planes, as in

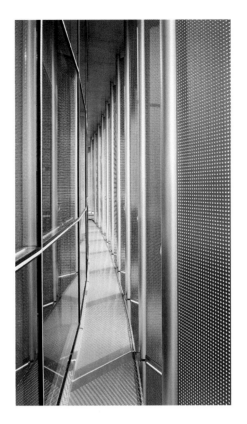

the junction of the roof plane with the body of the building, impart an almost manneristic divergence from what originated as quite stable planar compositions in the Iwasaki Museum and Maki's house.

Vital to the expression of the building are the junctions of its various planes. These occur where there are major shifts in the logic of the sections, such as the change in materials at the National Museum of Art from the rough stone of the podium to the polished stone of the sheathing walls, or in the sensitive play of different means of concrete processing and finishing as at the Guest House of Keio University, Shonan Fujisawa Campus. These shifts in materials, their finishing and their jointing, represent a further level of the expression of the intellectual order of the building.

Assemblage

Maki's fundamental approach to the assemblage of groups of buildings, as in "group form", continues as a characteristic of his compositions for single buildings of the 1970s, with the Iwasaki Museum providing an evident example. The axonometric of the Iwasaki Museum is of particular interest as it combines a forceful central spine with various attachments of differing spatial characteristics. These 1970s buildings are composed by assembling parts made up of simple geometric forms, but in later works Maki juxtaposes diverse irregular elements, as in the Zeebrugge Ferry Terminal project, 1989, where "four forms that suggest an iceberg, the wings of a bird, and the needle of a compass form an ensemble atop a disc floating in air".[24] Equally radical in the grouping of distinct parts is

the YKK Research Center that brings together the glass cage of the atrium, the curved glazed block of the offices, and other divergent aluminium-clad box-like blocks, all arranged about a central court space. Similar compositional principles can be seen in the Asahi Broadcasting Center.

Critical also in the composition of parts is Maki's interest in the space between elements – the *sukima* (residual space) as a cultural expression. He writes of the *sukima* as a powerful consideration: "When a building is given a particular locality, the *sukima* that results constitutes a mirror of the local culture in one sense or another. The city is an aggregate of such instances. What defines it is not the buildings themselves, but the entirety of the local community which contains them, and its characteristic structure – that's what

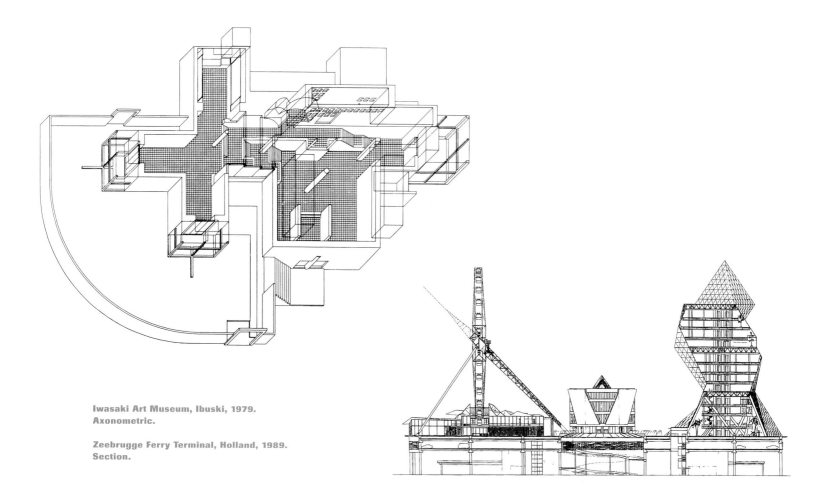

Iwasaki Art Museum, Ibuski, 1979.
Axonometric.

Zeebrugge Ferry Terminal, Holland, 1989.
Section.

the *sukima* is all about, and that's the relationship between a city and *sukima*."[25] The word "*sukima*" results from *suk* (meaning empty slit) and *ma* (the void between). *Sukima* is a literal thing – Maki talks of the 6-meter *sukima* between his building and an existing building at Rissho, and says that this would be intolerable in America as it is too close, and in England the buildings would join. Further, he comments that "when things are to be assembled together, there must be some principle at work, otherwise there would be no order. There could be several such principles, and I think that this *sukima* could be one of them."[26]

Clearly this mode of creating is a continuation of the assemblage of parts typical of the

sukiya style. These means of composing give rise to buildings that are rarely frontal in composition, normally being conceived as strongly three-dimensional in their interior space as well as their exterior form. Compatible with the above is the persistence of a balance of symmetry and asymmetry in the designs and of strong axial alignments in the planning with deviant paths within it. This is described by Jean-Louis Cohen as a "means of resolution that accommodates the local and partial symmetries, carefully considered within a general symmetry, that is understood by the introduction of anomalous elements into a centralised axial system".[27] These characteristics are common in these buildings; a clear example is provided by the Iwasaki Art Museum,

Stage I, where the major staired path moves to the side and up as well as along the principal longitudinal axis, establishing a subtle duality, resolved by the shared passage at the final landing. Countering this is the strict centrality of the cross-axis of the main gallery space.

There are exceptions to a seeming absence of symmetry and frontality. Spiral clearly has a single commanding facade due to its position between adjacent buildings, and Tepia, with the freedom of more land, is both frontal and cubical. The frontality of Spiral also results from Maki's unconventional approach to the design: in Spiral the facade was designed first, and functions accommodated in relation to it. As Maki says, "Function followed form."[28] At the National Museum of Modern Art, although

Iwasaki Art Museum, Ibuski, 1979.

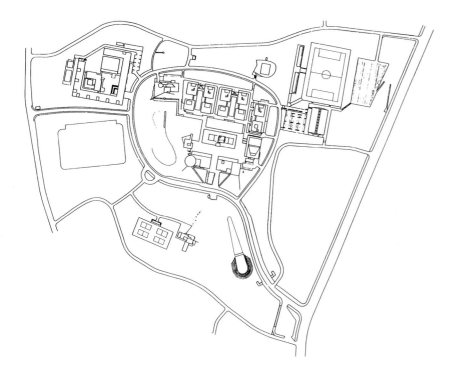

Keio University Shonan Campus, Fujisawa,
1992. Site plan.

YKK Guest House, Kurobe, 1982. Plan.

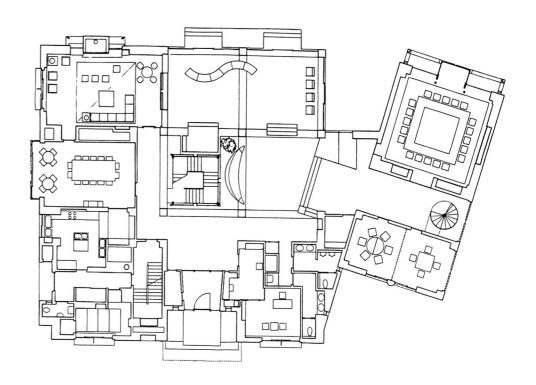

Kaze-no-Oka Crematorium, Nakatsu, 1996.

the plan and facades are regular rectangles, Maki rescues the facades from symmetry by deviations in the placement of openings. This is clear in the principal east facade where one large unbalanced square punctures the skin in the otherwise symmetrical composition. Further, although the buildings composed of an assemblage of parts are highly sculptural, segments of them are commandingly frontal and symmetrical, clear examples being the porch facades of the first stage of the Iwasaki Museum and the strongly centralised parts of the east facade of the YKK Guest House.

Maki tends to favour the introduction of skewed alignments within the controlling orderly framework of regular compositions. His usual design method is to study these angled compositions in models with the axial placements determined by the eye rather than by a certain predetermined angle. The displacements tend to favour 15, 17 or 18 degrees rather than the more regular 45 degrees. The strict orthogonal regularity of the Keio Shonan Campus is relieved by the angling of the Student Center to look along the lake located diagonally to the axis of the campus buildings. The volumes of Fujisawa Gymnasium and the angled conference room at the YKK Guest House provide earlier examples of such a shift. In this way Maki's work retains a sense of individuality with an intuitive, rather than a set geometric, determination of associations. He describes this mode of composition as arising from the interaction of two independent forms. At the YKK Guest House one was large and one was small: "Each body has symmetry and when they are together the composition is too heavy. In order to destroy the unfamiliarity between large and small, often, as here, I shift the axis."[29]

The tendency to displacement in Maki's architecture becomes visually explicit in the formal composition and torsion in the parts of the Kirishima Concert Hall. The Concert Hall is first viewed from above on the road from Kagoshima, as one looks down on the shining silver of the splayed, angled roof. The road then leads to below the site where the building is now viewed as somewhat precariously perched on its hillock site. The canted walls of the building lean forward over the drop, immediately imparting a sense of uneasiness. Further, access to the foyer along the northern side resulted in a displacement of the princi-

Toyota Guest House and Memorial Hall, Nagoya, 1974. Vignettes of the landscape.

Tepia, Tokyo, 1989. Plaza.

pal volume from the central axis of its podium, creating a sense of disturbance in an otherwise symmetrical composition. The principal drama of the building derives from the prominent shape of the displaced and twisted roof. This contrasts with the low, relaxed profiles of Maki's previous large metal roofs. Rather than giving a sense of repose, the roof at Kirishima appears tensely tied down, seeming to strain upwards. A marked displacement also occurs in the brick Funeral Hall of Kaze-no-Oka which dramatically tips, seeming to be sinking into the ground. These buildings extend the developing expression in Maki's architecture of the late 1980s towards one generated from the tension inherent in instabilities. The displacement evident in various aspects of the

design is reflective of Maki's understanding of contemporary life and the generally accepted current global theories of social displacement with the erosion of the stability of previously accepted truths and ways.

Landscape

The settings in which Maki's buildings are placed, and the connection between building and garden, provide another level of ordering. Usually Maki works in collaboration with a landscape designer. The landscapes tend to fall into various groups: gardens designed to be viewed from particular spaces within the building, sequential compositions as a part of an overall design of experience conceived as "movement space", frozen tableaus represent-

ing make-believe worlds set aside from the chaos of reality, and landscapes that provide geometric extensions to the building.

As Kuma points out, Maki's perception of nature belongs to the pictorial tradition stemming from Chinese garden design, where the building serves as a frame in which to see nature.[30] The combination of the framing and gazing of "landscape paintings" and the motion intrinsic to the "stroll garden", also deriving from Chinese precedent, extend the Japanese tradition of garden design into contemporary work. This approach is seen in its most refined manifestations in the Toyota Guest House and the Kaze-no-Oka Crematorium, where small vignettes of landscape, within and without, are revealed through careful-

Natori Performing Arts Center, Natori, 1997.

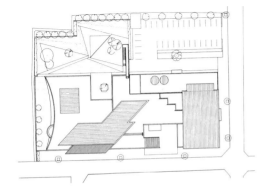

Nakatsu Obata Memorial Library, Nakatsu, 1993. Site plan.

Sandoz Pharmaceutical Research Institute, Tsukuba, 1993. Courtyard axonometric.

ly positioned openings as one moves through the building. It also occurs on the large scale as at the Kirishima Concert Hall which is designed to reveal the majestic volcanic range of its setting at the key moment before entering the major hall. Maki's use of "visibility modifiers" also belongs to the Chinese/Japanese tradition of garden design. That is, walls and screens, positioned outside the wall openings, control that which is seen and that which is not. These can be found in most of his work, including modest community buildings such as local halls and libraries, for example the Nakatsu Obata Memorial Library, 1993. The traditional courtyard is a further theme that appears consistently in Maki's designs, from the small court of his own house to large

transparent voids with singular clumps of planting as at the YKK Research Center and the Natori Performing Arts Center, 1997.

Also evident are the geometrically conceived surreal gardens such as that on the roof-top of Spiral, which proclaims its removal from the city, not only by location but by the contrivance of the design of its pyramid fountain, rigidly pruned conical Cyprus trees, and cylindrical bollards, which together present a toy-like French Renaissance garden. The inspiration here came from Le Corbusier's surreal roof garden for Apartment Charles de Beistegui, Paris, 1929–31. As Le Corbusier found that the roof-tops at Charles de Beistegui, the Marseilles Block, and at Chandigarh provided the only possible worlds for his pure Platonic

solids, so too Maki uses Spiral's roof as a remote plane on which to indulge in the fantasy of pure forms. Tepia's street-level plaza continues the stillness of the geometric games of Spiral's garden with a composition of chequered paving, cubic blocks and neatly clipped hedging, enlivened after work hours by the barrier of the vertical wall of ejected water that springs from the meandering watercourse which winds its way disturbing the frozen geometry of the composition.

More common in Maki's later work is the use of planting, paths and waterways as pattern – a three-dimensional carpet, like a chessboard, on which the buildings are arranged. In the Sandoz Pharmaceutical Research Institute, Tsukuba, 1993, Isar Büropark, Munich,

YKK Research Center, Tokyo, 1993. Courtyard.

Spiral, Tokyo, 1985. Roof-top garden.

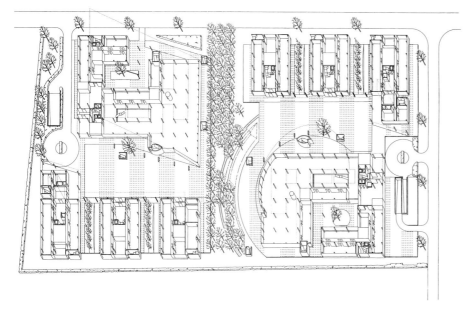

Isar Büropark, Munich, 1995. Axonometric.

1995, and the Natori Performing Arts Center, 1997, all designed with the landscape architect Tohru Mitain, geometric relationships are established between building and planting, and the order of the architecture is extended into the surrounding environs. At Sandoz Pharmaceutical Research Institute, a large courtyard with rows of azaleas and bamboo grass, and of mountain maple trees on a regular grid geometrically positioned in relation to the waterway, provides an orderly environment for the two bounding buildings. Isar Büropark, as the name suggests, is an assemblage of buildings in a park-like setting. Here the qualities of the surrounding area are abstracted and recreated in geometric pat-

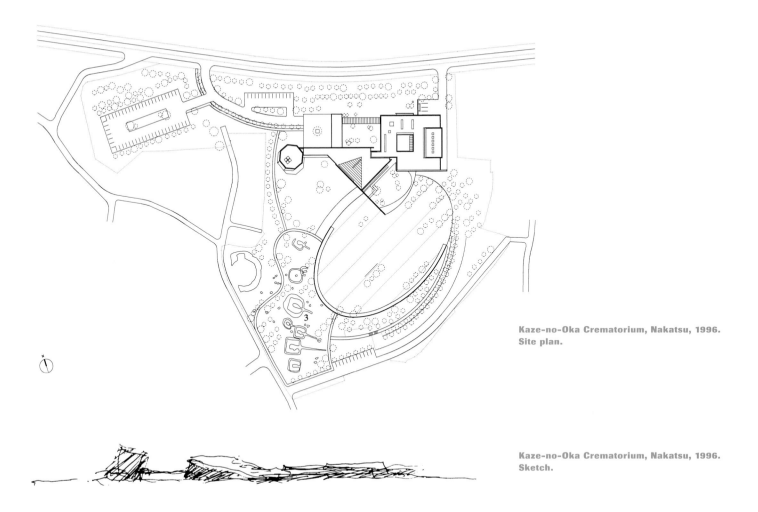

Kaze-no-Oka Crematorium, Nakatsu, 1996.
Site plan.

Kaze-no-Oka Crematorium, Nakatsu, 1996.
Sketch.

terns of lawns, paved surfaces and rows of maple trees. Alternate swathes of short and long grass mimic the surrounding agricultural farmlands. Similarly, in the project for the Tottori Prefectural Museum of Art rice paddies in the area served as inspiration for the terraced outside display areas, hence the Museum was proposed as a "garden art museum" linking inside and out. Within is a double-height glazed winter garden designed to return the visitor visually to the panoramic view of the landscape.

The Shimane Prefectural Museum of Archaeology and Ethnology, to be completed in 2005, is also designed to reflect and connect with its surroundings. The exterior Cor-

ten steel wall is a modern reference to the local smelting and metalcraft that once flourished there. From its interior platforms one can view the ancient Taisha Shrine and the mountainous landscape. The titanium roof surface easily blends into the surrounding scenery, creating an ever-changing skyline.

Inspired by Erik Gunnar Asplund's Woodland Chapel and Crematorium at Stockholm, 1940, the building and park setting of Kaze-no-Oka Crematorium provides an exceptional landscape in Maki's oeuvre.[31] On the hilltop, the abstract forms of the parts of the crematorium join multiple sculptural and symbolic forms which have been melded together to create an abstract tableau combining a pre-exist-

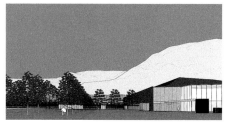

Shimane Prefectural Museum of Archaeology and Ethnology, Shimane, 2005.

Floating Pavilion, Groningen, Holland, 1996.

ing graveyard, third-century burial tumuli, and a hollowed-out grassed oval area with a central sunken pit containing wind-chimes by Yasuko Shono. The building-object and earth forms present an abstracted intervention with similar effect to the sculpture of Richard Serra and other artists whose work engages with the landscape.[32] From the middle of the sunken basin the surroundings are edited out by the embracing earth berms, and the haunting notes of the chimes fill the air, imparting a sense of peaceful solitude. In contrast, the most ethereal, yet the most transforming, of Maki's constructed elements is the Groningen Floating Pavilion, 1996, which has no site of its own but enters into dialogue with the ambience of the light and the setting at each loca-

tion where it stops. Apart from its fleeting beauty of cloud-like forms, it owes little to tradition but much to the dynamic present.

The engagement of Maki's buildings with their settings accords with the development in the architecture, from the contained podium buildings of the 1960s, lifted above and divorced from their settings, to Maki's interest in movement in the 1970s, and to the abstracted geometries of the 1980s, and to the more expansive buildings of his later work.

Imagery

One part of Maki's intention to extend the platform of modernism was to enrich it with a representative value, that is, to work with "a modernism that deals with images".[33] To this end

Maki employs both abstraction and allusion, with abstraction exploited to develop an attuned aesthetic for a technological future and coded references deployed to focus the general theme of the work. English words are commonly used as theme metaphors since, unlike Japanese words which have highly explicit meanings and connotations, they can be freely interpreted, allowing scope for lateral thinking. Examples used by Maki to evoke images include phrases such as "doll's house" and "ship's galley". Further, according to Watanabe, "What these words conjure up is what is important. Because they are in English they can be invested with other meanings, vague meanings."[34] Kuma explains, "The important thing is not to use the literal met-

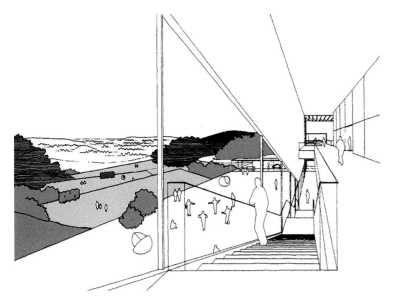

View to the sculpture terrace.

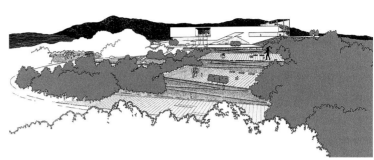

Building in its setting.

View from the winter garden.

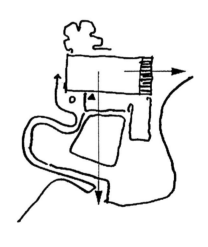

View axes.

Tottori Prefectural Museum of Art, Tottori City, 1998.

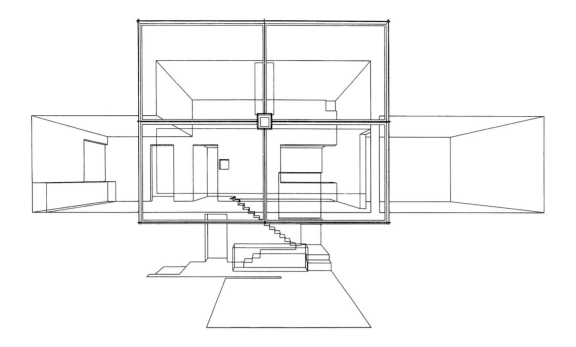

Volume and line symbols.

Maki House, Tokyo, 1978. Abstracted diagram.

aphor but to make Japanisation of the words. The metaphor is acceptable in Japanese culture because the metaphor has no form."[35]

Coding devices began to emerge clearly in Maki's architecture in the 1970s, and these would seem to belong to concerns with, first, images of stability (and later instability), second, references to both European and Japanese past architecture, third, signs of status and community value in public buildings, and, fourth, messages denoting the present state of the world.

Images of stability (and instability) – codes of tradition

Images of stability appear as abstract identifying symbols that mainly are integral to the building's exterior form. Images of stability are generally simple references such as iconic forms of shelter and enclosure, and are denoted principally by pictograms of house ele-

ments. The most commonly used are the geometric abstraction of a stepped pyramid form representing a squared-off roof and the cross symbolising the security of the cage and representing the square-window icon of the child's drawing.[36] This choice of markers provides an interesting parallel to Aldo Rossi's similar selection of the universal symbols of the triangular pediment and the cross-barred window. There is, however, a haunting quality to Rossi's symbols, which does not exist in the fresh clarity of Maki's marks. These signs are most explicit in the imagery of the late 1970s' buildings, such as the Maki Residence, and the first stage of the Iwasaki Museum. The square and cross signs persist, however, through all of Maki's architecture, and even appear in large buildings such as the New Keio Library, Mita Campus, where the intermediary cross-beams and posts form crosses on the first and second levels and "T"s on the third and fourth. Here

too the overall silhouette is Maki's house-roof image on an exaggerated scale.

The Iwasaki Museum extends its abstract referencing with blind porches permitting no exit, and over-scaled sculptural stairs not intending passage. The glazed light troughs over the galleries have further iconic value. Maki calls them "light rooms" and reads them as somewhat symbolic of the purpose of the building – a position that is additional to a pragmatic reading of function. The literal use of a child-like house image is to be seen in Maki's project at Cracow for a foster home to accommodate a family of eight orphans under the care of one mother. The house, with a bigger upper portion, is figuratively expressive of the unusual group living within the dwelling.

The "house" imagery, clearly that of the English country manor, establishes the exterior character of the YKK Guest House at Kurobe. The building has a sophistication

New Library for Keio University, Mita Campus, Tokyo, 1985. Elevation.

quite distinct from the innocence of the Cracow house. This is a house on the grand scale, with symbolic pitched roofs, towering chimney and vertical ribbons of bay windows. Here Maki ran the risk of pushing over the frontiers into kitsch, but with his customary restraint and the elegance of the proportions and the geometry of the composition, the building emerged instead as one of his most refined and engaging designs.

The Japanese house as well as the Western manor provided a starting point for the design of the YKK Guest House. The entry hall calls to mind the lower entrances of the traditional house, and the squared pattern of blond timbers against translucent panels clearly is derivative of *shoji* screens or paper lanterns. Further, this central hall, three storeys high, with large intersecting concrete beams above, generates a space and structure strongly reminiscent of the entry halls to the

grand traditional houses of cities such as Kanazawa.[37]

The Iwasaki Art Museum's two-volume mode of organisation related to the two stages of the building program, the first of 1979, with the annex of 1987. The use of the Japanese house as a grounding for design is most evident in the play between the contrasting sources of the first and second stages. Whereas the first building has the form and clarity of a Palladian villa, the annex (connected to the first by an underground passageway) is heavy and shrouded and tells of the darkness of the farmhouse. Stage I houses the owner's private collection of Japanese modern art and Western Fauvist paintings, whereas the annex shows the collection of Japanese ceramics, painting and folk art. Various moods and lighting effects accompany the different exhibitions. The entry hall is suggestive of the *doma* work area of the house with a floor of earthy

Iwasaki Art Museum, Ibuski, 1987. Stage II.
Entry exibition hall.

Iwasaki Art Museum, Ibuski, 1979. Porch.

Iwasaki Art Museum, Ibuski, 1979. Light
rooms.

materials, free-standing columns, minimal openings and heavy roofs, while the principal exhibition room plays the part of the *zashiki*, reception room, and uses glass blocks and light *shoji* screens. The movement path here climbs up through the galleries and finally breaks out into the light and view on the highest level. This route with its rooms of varying moods and fitness for occasion would seem to contain the seeds of the sequences of the Kaze-no-Oka Crematorium of 1996.

These simple geometric buildings, which embrace the language of a picturesque adaptation of the familiar, are charged with an appealing formal and iconographic quality that extends beyond conventional readings of modern architecture. This is a revealing and reassuring architecture, familiar and sheltering.

References to tradition and familiar objects are found throughout Maki's work anchoring it in place and Japanese history. Boats figure frequently as metaphors. The Iwasaki Museum was originally charged with the image of a ship, the Kirishima Concert Hall was envisaged as a ship, and ship imagery helped give

form to the Yerba Buena Gardens Visual Arts Center, San Francisco. Maki describes the project for the Palazzo del Cinema, Venice, 1990, as resembling "a crystalline boat floating silently on the surface of the water".[38] The side elevation of the International Convention Center, Niigata, 2003, resembles an ocean liner. And, of course, there is the actual boat-stage for Groningen, 1996.

Spiral, Tokyo, and the Museum of Modern Art, Kyoto, are highly descriptive of place. Spiral with its chaotic patterns captures the dynamic of Tokyo, and the Kyoto Museum is sober and balanced and with a dignity appropriate to the more measured rhythms of that gridded city. The Museum has numerous allusions extending from reference to the rusticated stonework of Japanese monumental masonry, to the heroic form and symmetry of the massive red Torri Gate at its door marking

entry to the Heian Shrine in Okazaki Park, and to the corner stair towers that light up as paper lanterns at night. Striking is the classical use of materials, notably granite, selected by Maki because of its eternal nature.

The use of symbolic and literal references to common objects also extends into Maki's large structures. He writes that the inspiration for the space of the main arena of the 1985 Fujisawa Gymnasium lay in the "ceramic Nambu-ware pot, the *shamisen* plectrum, and fans",[39] with its form suggesting a *mokugyo* (wood blocks Buddhist priests strike while reading sutras), but to an even greater extent the helmet of a samurai. For Maki, one of architecture's roles is to remind one of subconscious shapes. He writes that Fujisawa's roof "suggests both the past and the future by evoking at the same time both a medieval knight's helmet and a spaceship".[40] Such a

connection is made explicit with the remarkable sketch depicting a virtual transfiguration of a helmet form into the roof shape of the second stadium. This drawing is among the most descriptive images, capturing the vital blending and transformation of tradition into the present and the future. Maki speaks of the roof "as a cultural artefact, as a *constructed* artefact that stands in a complex relationship to history. In this way I believe it is possible to see the roof itself as a metaphor for the coming together of two traditions."[41] But much of the imagery of Fujisawa came from its making. As Maki points out, "The handcrafted welding of the stainless steel sheets is probably not that much different than what was required for making a suit of armour."[42] But Maki's intentions often go further than simply revealing. At Fujisawa he sought a futuristic image, and in this context he refers to the Zep-

Fujisawa Gymnasium, Fujisawa, 1984.
Collage image of the subarena under
construction.

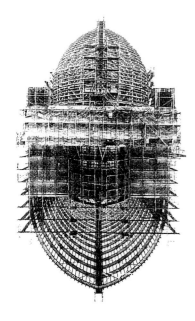

pelins he saw as a child – the excitement of a new era to a child's imagination and the appeal of "something different", "something strange". At Fujisawa the strange shapes were intended to arouse awe, as "familiar scenery in the city reminds us of a common past; it provides comfort and stability. Unfamiliar scenery, on the other hand, provokes both fear and excitement, and in the process unleashes our power of imagination."[43] This search for an architecture that resonates with the new age is a common ingredient in Maki's architecture. He explains this as: "Suppose there is a new need and we have responded with a certain special idea, produced it, and people, not knowing what the building is, are moved by seeing it or being inside it, then it might have achieved something. So that is something for which we are always looking."[44] So Maki's symbols of this time ranged from those that

spoke of the known and the familiar to those evocative of the unknown and uncanny.

Public presence

Public architecture, in the Western sense, is a new concept in Japan. The culture has always been concerned with that which is hidden rather than that which is evident. Even what might be considered a public building, such as the Emperor's palace, is screened from public gaze. Maki writes, "Even in Japanese contemporary architecture, public character is expressed through the use and design of territory – in the sensitivity to borders, both marked and unmarked; in the multiple layering of space by means of *shoji* and other screens; and in spatial arrangements structured not by the idea of a center but by the idea of depth *(oku)*."[45] The question as to what might be an appropriate expression of public

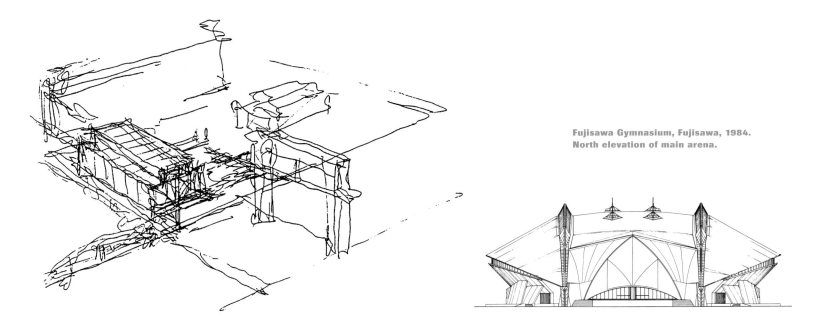

Fujisawa Gymnasium, Fujisawa, 1984.
North elevation of main arena.

National Museum of Modern Art, Kyoto, 1986. Sketch.

building in the new Japan was fraught with conceptual challenges.

In the 1980s, Maki wrote at some length on what he saw as public architecture and its role, and Maki's and Isozaki's responses to this issue provided the material for the Japan Society's exhibition "New Public Architecture: Recent Projects by Fumihiko Maki and Arata Isozaki" at Japan House, New York, in 1985.[46] In a revealing essay published in the exhibition catalogue Maki discusses the need for a public architecture. He writes that "public" here "refers to a *character* that certain buildings ought to possess ... a public dimension", and "the most necessary condition for architecture, particularly for public architecture, is that its spaces, or at least its major spaces, have a dignity and ceremonial quality."[47] Demonstrative of these principles is the National Museum of Modern Art, Kyoto, Maki's major civic institution of this period, which was displayed in the "New Public Architecture" exhibition. In the catalogue the building is described as being concerned with fit and decorum, using hierarchies of scale and sym-

metrical elevational and plan matrices in its organisation, having a grammatically "classical" plan and relationship to the volumetric organisation, and embodying a power of abstraction and a relevance to traditional Japanese cultural values expressed in such elements as the translucent *shoji*-like corner stairwells and the grid pattern of the facade. Further, its strong public presence is pronounced in the solemnity of its simple rectangular form, the basically symmetrical facades, its classical tripartite elevations, its heavy rusticated base, its refined use of elegant materials, and, in the interior, by the grandeur of the foyer with its stair, for, as Maki claims, public buildings need spaces that have dignity "acquired by a certain spatial play and by an imposing appearance".[48]

To pronounce its national stature, Maki drew on the historical setting in Kyoto, and the uncommon gridded plan of the city streets is echoed in the lines of the building's form and surfaces. Further contributing to its special nature is the Museum's location at the entrance to Japan's earliest modern park,

Niigata Center, Niigata, 2003.

Okazaki Park, containing the Heian Shrine. The National Museum of Modern Art is but one example of many in which Maki attempted to address the problem of an appropriate presence for a public building, in a country without evident precedent, through the classic forms of the Western tradition.

Time

The representation of the situation of the present in a global context, and in the particular circumstances of late twentieth-century Japan, is critical to Maki's architecture. So Maki continues in the spirit of the modern with the intent to respond to and encapsulate the "spirit of the times" – the zeitgeist. This is clearly evident in the "classic" buildings of the 1970s and 1980s in Japan – years of invention and prosperity. Maki sees it as a duty and responsibility of the architect to express the unique circumstance of the building industry in Japan. He states, "I believe architecture makes a valuable contribution to society by using available technology and craftsmanship to the fullest and thereby creating a work that is

truly representative of the times, and to understand such a task is the responsibility of the architect."[49] The particular qualities of Tepia, which is devoted to the display of advanced electronic and micro-electronic products, derive from Maki's determination that it would exhibit the state-of-the-moment of the art, and beyond. Hence Tepia embodies the most advanced technologies and materials available. It indicates the high-water mark of Japanese building technology in the 1990s, and is seen by Maki as a testimony to modern society. An achievement of Maki's architecture lies in providing both global and local readings of the state of culture and technology without recourse to overt regional or stylistic representation.

But the times are more than technology, and few buildings are more expressive of the general tenor of a place at a particular time than Spiral. Spiral was commissioned by the Wacoal lingerie company as an image for the company and as a contribution to the life of the people of Tokyo. Maki had a virtually open brief, and produced an elegant, but not elite,

building of pleasure – even indulgence. Spiral, with restaurants, an art arena, speciality shops, luxury boutiques, beauty shop and theater etc., contains a plethora of relaxing and gratifying places. The building involves a process of wrapping with layers of sheets that have to be penetrated sequentially before the contents are revealed. Spiral provides a masterly incarnation of Japan of the 1980s, for in being a source of gratification it is reflective of the inflated economy, of the rampant consumerism of the 1980s, and of the search for novelty by the over-sated Japanese buyer. Further, it is fitting of its place and time in the vitality and contextualism of its facade, capturing the very essence of the elements, patterns and tempo of the bustling Tokyo of its day. In addition, it cleverly combines a witty high art with the mess of the street vernacular to produce an arresting and involving image balanced on a knife edge. The building artistically blends references to the traditional past, the modern past (notably Le Corbusier) and the immediate present in the spatial as well as material considerations of its

Spiral, Tokyo, 1985.

composition. The syncopating facade of Spiral is one of the major examples of public art in Japan of the 1980s. In all, Spiral is one of the most potent and expressive buildings of Maki's career, and of its time.[50]

In this way the "classic" buildings responded to the representational demands placed upon them, graphically providing an index to the state of the environment, the state of culture and the state of industry in Japan at the height of its boom period.

Maki's buildings exhibit an enrichment of architecture going beyond the limits of orthodox modernism. His "classic" buildings provide a subtle freedom yet retain the marks of recognisable, dependable shelter. They demonstrate that modern architecture is capable of extension into fresh interpretative realms, and of sustaining and evoking the spirit of the contemporary world.[51] There is a sense of refined rebellion in the work as it evolves from the quiet classicism of the

Iwasaki Museum to the engaged exuberance of Spiral, the technological sophistication of Tepia, the restrained monumentality of the National Museum of Modern Art, to the quiet composure of Triad. Through his buildings and writings, Maki attempts to invigorate a tired modernity by seeking empowering orders that accommodate the complexities of the time, and an enhanced representative strength in order to endow the buildings with appropriate meanings.

Triad, Hotaka, Nagano, 2002. Overview showing laboratory.

Notes

1 Fumihiko Maki, "Introduction", in Botond Bognar, *Togo Murano: Master Architect of Japan*, New York, Rizzoli, 1996, p. 21.

2 Fumihiko Maki, "Complexity and Modernism", *Space Design*, 1 (340), 1993, p. 7. This is an important article in which Maki sets forth his intentions at this time.

3 Fumihiko Maki, "A visit to Junzo Yoshimura's mountain lodge", *The Japan Architect*, 47, 12 (192), December 1972, p. 102. Robert Venturi, *Complexity and Contradiction in Architecture*, New York, Museum of Modern Art, 1966, p. 102.

4 Hiroyuki Suzuki, "Context and manner in the works of Fumihiko Maki", *The Japan Architect*, 54, 5 (265), May 1979, p. 81.

5 Conversation with Kengo Kuma, Tokyo, 1995.

6 Martin Spring, "Nippon Convention Center", *The Japan Architect*, 65, 8/9 (400–401), August/September 1990, p. 50.

7 Fumihiko Maki, "My encounter with Modernism", unpublished manuscript translated by Hiroshi Watanabe.

8 Conversation with Hiroyuki Suzuki, Tokyo, 1995.

9 David B. Stewart, "Architecture and the beholder. Five new works by Fumihiko Maki", *Space Design*, 1 (256), 1986, p. 115.

10 Fumihiko Maki, "Architecture and communication", *Space Design*, 1 (424), 2000, p. 7.

11 Fumihiko Maki, *Fragmentary Figures: The Collected Architectural Drawings*, Tokyo, Kyuryudo Art Publishing Co. Ltd, 1989.

12 Fumihiko Maki, "Sketches", *Fumihiko Maki: A Presence Called Architecture – Report from the Site*, Gallery Ma Books, Catalogue for an exhibition for Gallery MA, Tokyo, TOTO Shuppan, 1996, p. 19.

13 Conversation with Hiroyuki Suzuki, Tokyo, 1995.

14 Maki, "Complexity and Modernism", p. 7.

15 Maki, "Complexity and Modernism", p. 7.

16 Fumihiko Maki, *Details by Maki and Associates: Tepia*, Tokyo, Kajima Institute Publishing, 1991, p. 7.

17 Heinrich Engel, *The Japanese House: A Tradition for Contemporary Architecture*, Tokyo, Charles E. Tuttle, 1964, p. 431.

18 Norman F. Carver, *Form and Space of Japanese Architecture*, Tokyo, Shokokusha, 1955, p. 135.

19 Conversation with Hiroshi Watanabe, Tokyo, 1995.

20 Maki's sketches are well recorded in *Fragmentary Figures: The Collected Architectural Drawings*.

21 David B. Stewart, "Lightness", *The Japan Architect*, 65, 8/9 (400/401), August/September 1990, pp. 26–33.

22 Maki, *Fragmentary Figures*, (no pagination).

23 This glass was later used at Hillside West and the MIT Media Laboratories.

24 Maki, "Complexity and Modernism", p. 7.

25 Fumihiko Maki and Hiroshi Hara, "Dialogue: Hiroshi Hara + Fumihiko Maki (Summary)", *Space Design*, 6 (177), 1979, Frontispiece: Japanese version, pp. 141–152.

26 Fumihiko Maki and Hiroshi Hara, "Dialogue: Hiroshi Hara + Fumihiko Maki (Summary)".

27 Jean-Louis Cohen, "The recent work of Fumihiko Maki beyond the fragment: Time regained", *The Japan Architect,* 16, Special Issue on Fumihiko Maki, Winter 1994, p. 184.

28 Maki, *Fragmentary Figures,* (no pagination).

29 Conversation with Maki, Tokyo, 1995.

30 Conversation with Kengo Kuma, Tokyo, 1995.

31 Toru Mitani is Professor of Landscape Architecture at Shiga Prefectural University.

32 For example, Serra's Schunnemuk Fork of 1991.

33 Fumihiko Maki, "New directions in Modernism", *Space Design,* 1 (256), 1986, p. 7.

34 Conversation with Hiroshi Watanabe, Tokyo, 1995.

35 Conversation with Kengo Kuma, Tokyo, 1995.

36 This iconic quality of Maki's buildings of this time is well discussed in Serge Salat and Françoise Labbé (eds.), "An aesthetic of fragmentation", *Fumihiko Maki: An Aesthetic of Fragmentation,* New York, Rizzoli, 1988, pp. 19–33. The stepped pyramid image is particularly suggestive in Japan where a second level is commonly present over the center portion of the house.

37 Two of these concrete beams defining the space are structurally redundant.

38 Fumihiko Maki, *Fumihiko Maki: Buildings and Projects,* New York, Princeton Architectural Press, 1997, p. 88.

39 Fumihiko Maki, "The public dimension in contemporary architecture", in A. Munroe (ed.), *New Public Architecture: Recent Projects by Fumihiko Maki and Arata Isozaki,* Catalogue for exhibition, New York, Japan Society, 1985.

40 Fumihiko Maki, "City, image, materiality", in *Fumihiko Maki: An Aesthetic of Fragmentation,* p. 12.

41 Fumihiko Maki, "The roof at Fujisawa", *Fumihiko Maki: Buildings and Projects,* p. 153.

42 Maki, "The public dimension in contemporary architecture", p. 19.

43 Fumihiko Maki, *Selected Passages on the City and Architecture,* internal publication of Maki and Associates, Tokyo, 2000, p. 19.

44 Conversation with Maki, Tokyo, 1995.

45 Maki, "The public dimension in contemporary architecture", p. 19.

46 See Maki, "The public dimension in contemporary architecture".

47 Maki, "The public dimension in contemporary architecture", p. 19.

48 Maki, "The public dimension in contemporary architecture", p.19.

49 Fumihiko Maki, "Introduction" *The Japan Architect,* 65, 8/9 (400/401), August/September 1990, p. 9.

50 The historian Marc Treib comments that the facade of Spiral is the finest facade of the twentieth century. Conversation with Marc Treib, Tokyo, 2001.

51 Maki addresses these issues in a series of important essays, including Fumihiko Maki, "Modernism at the crossroad", *The Japan Architect,* 58, 3 (311), March 1983, pp. 18–22; Fumihiko Maki, "New directions in Modernism", *Space Design,* 1 (256), 1986, pp. 6–7; Fumihiko Maki, "Complexity and Modernism", pp. 6–7.

Triad: Conceptual sketch.

9 Weaving: Thread and Strand

Space, City, Order, Making – these are recurrent themes that have engaged the thinking and the pencil of Fumihiko throughout his career. Space has been continually addressed as the matter of architecture, the city as architecture's central responsibility, order as that which gives form, and making as that which materialises the intentions. These we can view as threads continuously present in Maki's mind. With these threads he creates a woven strand, the cross section of which becomes a piece of architecture at each particular time. It is an open-ended strategy whereby he carefully selects and unifies elements that have been accumulated throughout the years of his practice. Depending on the site, the brief, and the intellectual and technological stages of the date of the project, various threads will assume greater importance ("thickness") over others, and may adopt different characteristics which will identify the work as being of a new era. For example, the roof of the research

laboratory of Triad, 2001, belongs to the same family as that of the Fujisawa Gymnasium, 1984, but the thinness of the protruding portion of the curved wall and the canopy of the roof gallery is the result of a very sophisticated technology and craftsmanship only available at present which imparts an appearance of the spirit of the time, not the 1980s. Such detail changes are significant in determining the whole character of the complex. So while the threads may be ever present, their effect and contribution to the design outcome will be determined by the evolving circumstances. In this way Maki's work demonstrates a continuing commitment and concern, yet each new project holds ever-renewed relevance.

This ability to weave past discoveries, accumulated during years of exploration, with new eventualities has allowed Maki to retain his position as one of the major creative figures in international architecture. Since the 1960s, he has kept modern architecture alive,

and has continually regenerated and extended it with a fresh spirit suited to the moods and demands of shifting times. Strangely, at any point in time he has emerged as one of the most consistent architects world-wide, yet one of the most innovative. To modern architecture he has brought an unmatched touch of delicacy, elegance and sophistication. For the new millennium, Maki is designing some of the finest work of his lifelong contribution to international architecture.

Glossary of Japanese Terms

doma	an earth floor often found in entry spaces and kitchens in traditional houses
hiroba	an open space; a public square.
kanji	literally "Chinese script". This is the traditional, originally Chinese script of ideographic characters which was taken up by the Japanese and subsequently modified. Kanji is combined in written Japanese with two collections of syllabic phonetic systems: *hiragana* is used to write Japanese words, while *katakana* is generally employed to render foreign words into Japanese. Some elements of Latin script are also employed.
ma	an interval; a pause; a rest.
meisho	a famous place; a place of interest. First, they were places where cultured people met and read poetry while appreciating scenery. Then later, they became places of festivals, particularly in shrines or temple compounds. Meisho derives from the Edo period. While still strictly delineated, it was of a more public nature than the spaces previously available to the general populace.
mokugyo	a wooden block as found in Buddhist temples.
nagare	to flow (this is a noun taken from the verb *Nagareru*).
niwa	a garden; a courtyard; a semi-public space.
oku	the inner part; the heart; the depth.
shamisen	three-stringed plucked lute originally associated with the urban world of the pleasure quarters and theaters of the Edo period. It is a wooden instrument with cat or dog skin covering the front and back of the body. Shamisen notation denotes intervals rather than pitches.
shoin	style of residential architecture. Shoin means "library" or "study" and the style came to be widely used both in temple living quarters and guest halls and in the mansions of the military. Developing out of the classic *shinden* style, shoin-zukuri still serves as the prototype for the today's traditional-style Japanese houses.
shoji	sliding panels of rice paper with light timber framing members serving to create translucent screens that are used to enclose and divide rooms.
sukima	a residual space; a slit of space, a crack; a chink; an opening.
sukiya	style of residential architecture; literally sukiya denotes a building in which tea ceremony was performed. Sukiya-zukuri is a style incorporating features characteristic of the sukiya.
tatami	a tightly packed stiff rice-straw mat, approximately 910 x 1,820 mm in size. Tatami mats, which are abutted to cover the floor, are one of the most distinctive features of the Japanese house.
zashiki	a reception room (as in a formal dining/lounge/entertainment room in a house) commonly with tatami mats on a wooden floor.

Biography

1928   Born in Tokyo

Professional Career

1954–55   Designer, Skidmore Owings and Merrill, New York, New York

1955–58   Designer, Sert Jackson and Associates, Cambridge, Massachusetts

1956–58   Associate, Campus Planning Office, Washington University, St Louis, Missouri

1958–65   Consultant for a number of offices in the United States and Japan

1965–   Principal, Maki and Associates

1987–90   Member, International Committee of the Japan Institute of Architects

Teaching and Research

1956–58   Assistant Professor, Washington University, St Louis

1958–60   Graham Foundation Fellow 1960–62 Associate Professor, Washington University,St Louis

1962–65   Associate Professor, Graduate School of Design, Harvard University, Cambridge, Mass.

1965–79   Visiting critic, lecturer, professor at a number of universities internationally

1979–89   Professor, University of Tokyo

1993–95   Visiting Lecturer, School of Environmental Information, Keio University

Awards

1963   Japan Institute of Architecture (for Toyoda Memorial Hall)

1969   Mainichi Art Prize (for Rissho University Kumagaya Campus)

1973   The 24th Art Prize from Ministry of Education (for Hillside Terrace)

1980   Japan Art Prize (for Hillside Terrace)

1985   Japan Institute of Architecture (for Fujisawa Municipal Gymnasium)

1987   Honorary Doctor's Degree in Art and Architecture, Washington University, St Louis

1987   Reynolds Memorial Award (for Spiral Building)

1988   Wolf Prize, Israel

1988   Chicago Architecture Award

1990   Thomas Jefferson Medal in Architecture, Charlottesville, Virginia

1991   The 5th International Design Award, Osaka

1993   The Pritzker Architecture Prize

1993   Gold Medal, International Union of Architects

1993   Prince of Wales in Urban Design, Harvard University, Cambridge, Mass. (for Hillside Terrace)

1993   Quarternario '93 International Award for Innovative Technology in Architecture (for Makuhari Messe)

1993   The Asahi Prize, Asahi Shimbun Foundation

1994   Asia Pacific Distinguished Architectural Scholar, Honolulu, Hawaii

1995   Concrete Architecture Prize, Swedish Concrete Institute

1997   Togo Murano Memorial Award (for Kaze-no-Oka Crematorium)

1998   Officier de l'ordre des arts et des lettres, France

1999   Arnold Brunner Memorial Prize in Architecture, American Academy of Arts and Sciences

1999   The Praemium Imperiale, The Japan Arts Association

Exhibitions

1980	"Late Entries to the Chicago Tribune Tower Competition": Contemporary Art, Chicago
1983	"Three Projects in Progress": Axis Gallery, Tokyo
1983–85	"Architecture in Paris": United States Tour
1984	"Styrian Autumn": Graz, Austria
1984	"Japan Architecture International, Rotterdam": Rotterdam, Netherlands
1985	"Recent Projects of Fumihiko Maki": Tony Tower, Osaka
1985	"Paris Biennale": La Grande Halle de la Villette, Paris
1985	"New Public Architecture: Recent Projects by Fumihiko Maki & Arata Isozaki": Gallery, New York
1987	"Tokyo Form & Spirit": Walker Art Center, Minneapolis, MoMA New York, MoMA San Francisco
1987–91	"Recent Projects": Paris, Venice, Rome, Genoa, Zurich, Graz, Berlin, Stuttgart, Antwerp, Copenhagen, Freiberg
1989	"Zeebrugge Sea Ferry Terminal Proposals": Royal Academy of Art, London
1989	"European Japan": Brussels, Belgium
1989	"Architecture Shaping the Future": University of California at San Diego
1990–91	"Architecture in Place": University of Virginia, Charlottesville; Philadelphia, New York, RIBA, London
1991	"Proposals for the Kyoto Concert Hall Competition": Japanese Pavilion, Venice Biennale
1991	"Proposals for the Palazzo del Cinema, Venezia": Italian Pavilion, Venice Biennale
1992	"Hillside Terrace Retrospective Exhibition": Hillside Terrace, Tokyo
1993	"Hillside Terrace 1967–1992": Harvard University, Cambridge, Mass.
1993	"Gold Medallist Retrospective Exhibition": AIA Convention, Chicago
1995	"Light Construction": Museum of Modern Art, New York
1996	"A Presence Called Architecture – A Report from the Site": Gallery MA, Tokyo
1997	"Architecture in Japan – Tradition in the Future": The Academy of Fine Arts, Vienna
1997	"From the Sublime to the Meticulous": Taipei Fine Art Museum, Taipei
1997	"Cities on the Move": Secession, Vienna
1998	"Japan 2000 Architecture for the Japanese Public": The Art Institute of Chicago, Chicago
1998	"The Construction of Scenery": Hillside Terrace, Tokyo
1998	"The Recent Projects": The Museum of Fine Art, Mexico City
1999	"Pritzker Architecture Prize 1979–1999": The Art Institute of Chicago, Chicago
1999	"Exhibition of Works by New Members and Recipients of Awards": Academy of Arts and Letters, New York
1999	"Making of the Public Realm – From Three Recent Projects": Borusan Culture and Art Center, Istanbul
1999	"Three Recent Projects": Tohoku University of Art and Design, Yamagata
1999	"Shenyang Forum International Urban Planning and Architecture": Urban Planning & Design Institute, China
1999	"4th International Biennial of Architecture in Brazil": Pavihao, Ciccillo Matarazzo, São Paolo
2001	"Fumihiko Maki: Modernity and the Construction of Scenery": Victoria and Albert Museum, London

Selected Projects

1960	Steinberg Arts Center, Washington University, St Louis, Missouri
1962	Nagoya University Toyoda Memorial Hall, Nagoya
1962	Chiba University Memorial Auditorium, Chiba
1966	Rinkai Center Building, Osaka
1966−92	Hillside Terrace Apartment Complex, Phases I−VI, Shibuya-ku, Tokyo
1968	Rissho University, Kumagaya Campus, Kumagaya, Saitama
1969	Senri Civic Center Building, Senri, Osaka
1969	Mogusa Town Center, Tokyo
1970	Senboku Archeological Museum, Senboku, Osaka
1971	Kanazawa Ward Office, Kanazawa, Yokohama
1972	St Mary's International School, Setagaya-ku, Tokyo
1972	Kato Gakuen Elementary School, Numazu, Shizuoka
1972	Osaka Prefectural Sports Center, Takaishi, Osaka
1973	Hiroo Homes & Towers, Minato-ku, Tokyo
1974	Tsukuba Academic New Town, Tsukuba, Ibaraki
1974	Toyota Guest House and Memorial Hall, Toyoda, Aichi
1974	Nobe Kindergarten, Yokohama, Kanagawa
1975	Public Housing Project, Lima, Peru
1975	Embassy of Japan, Brazil
1975	Marine Life Park for Expo '75 (National Aquarium), Okinawa
1976	Austrian Embassy, Minato-ku, Tokyo
1978	Kanazawa Seaside Town, Kanazawa, Kanagawa
1978	Namiki Elementary School, Kanazawa, Kanagawa
1979	Iwasaki Art Museum, Ibusuki, Kagoshima
1979	Royal Danish Embassy, Shibuya, Tokyo
1980	Kawawa Lower Secondary School, Yokohama, Kanagawa
1981	Toranomon NN Building, Minato-ku, Tokyo
1981	Mitsubishi Bank, Hiroo Branch, Minato-ku, Tokyo
1981	Kyoto Craft Center ABL, Higashiyama-ku, Kyoto
1981	Keio University Library, Mita Campus, Minato-ku, Tokyo
1982	Kota Kinabalu Sports Center, Sabah, East Malaysia
1982	YKK Guest House, Kurobe, Toyama
1982	Renovation of the Former Keio University, Mita Campus, Minato-ku, Tokyo
1983	Dentsu Advertising Building, Kita-ku, Osaka
1984	Minami Osawa Housing Project, Tama New Town, Hachioji, Tokyo
1984	Garden Plaza, Hiroo, Minato-ku, Tokyo
1984	Fujisawa Municipal Gymnasium, Fujisawa, Kanagawa
1985	West Plaza, Yokohama Central Station, Yokohama, Kanagawa
1985	Keio University Graduate School, Mita Campus, Minato-ku, Tokyo
1985	Spiral, Minato-ku, Tokyo
1985	Keio University Hiyoshi Library, Yokohama, Kanagawa
1986	National Museum of Modern Art, Sakyo-ku, Kyoto
1987	Iwasaki Art Museum Annex, Ibusuki, Kagoshima
1988	Tsuda Hall, Shibuya-ku, Tokyo
1989	Dai-Tokyo Fire & Marine Insurance Shinjuku Building, Shibuya-ku, Tokyo
1989	Toyama, Shimin Plaza, Toyama
1989	Tepia, Minato-ku, Tokyo
1989	Nippon Convention Center (Makuhari Messe), Chiba
1990	Tokyo Metropolitan Gymnasium, Shibuya-ku, Tokyo
1992	Keio University, Shonan Campus, Fujisawa, Kanagawa
1993	Nakatsu Obata Memorial Library, Nakatsu, Oita
1993	Sandoz Pharmaceutical Research Institute, Tsukuba, Ibaraki
1993	YKK Research Center, Sumida-ku, Tokyo
1993	Yerba Buena Gardens, Visual Arts Center, San Francisco, California
1994	Graduate School Research Center Keio University, Shonan Campus, Fujisawa, Kanagawa
1994	Seminar Guest House Keio University, Fujisawa Campus, Fujisawa, Kanagawa
1994	Kirishima International Concert Hall, Makizono, Kagoshima
1995	Isar Büropark, Munich, Germany
1995	Tokyo Church of Christ, Shibuya-ku, Tokyo
1996	Floating Pavilion, Groningen, Netherlands
1996	Kaze-no-Oka Crematorium, Nakatsu, Oita
1996	Fukuoka University Student Center, Jonan-ku, Fukuoka
1996	Kanagawa University Auditorium, Yokohama, Kanagawa
1997	District Community & Care Center, Yokohama, Kanagawa
1997	Natori Performing Arts Center, Natori, Miyagi
1998	Nippon Convention Center (Makuhari Messe), Phase 11, Chiba
1998	Hillside Terrace West, Shibuya-ku, Tokyo
1999	Toyama International Congress Center, Toyama
2000	Fukushima Prefectural Women's Center, Nihonmatsu, Fukushima
2001	Bürogebäude in Düsseldorf-Hafen, Düsseldorf, Germany
2002	Triad, Hotaka, Nagano
2002	Fukui Prefectural Library and Archives, Fukui
2002	ITE, Singapore
2003	Yokohama Bayside Tower, Yokohama, Kanagawa
2003	Asahi Broadcast Center, Minato-ku, Tokyo
2003	MIT Media Laboratory Expansion, Cambridge, Massachusetts
2003	Niigata International Convention Center, Niigata
2005	Visual Arts and Design Center, Washington University, St Louis
2005	Shimane Prefectural Museum of Archaeology and Ethnology, Shimane

Selected Bibliography

Selected writings by and on Fumihiko Maki

Kikutake, K., N. Kawazoe, M. Ohtaka, F. Maki and N. Kurokawa, *Metabolism: The Proposals for New Urbanism,* Tokyo, Bijutsu Shuppansha, 1960.

Maki, Fumihiko, (in part with jerry Goldberg), *Investigations in Collective Form,* St Louis, The School of Architecture, Washington University, 1964.

Maki, Fumihiko, *Movement Systems in the City,* Cambridge, Mass., Graduate School of Design, Harvard University, 1965.

Maki, Fumihiko, and Masato Ohtaka, "Some Thoughts on Collective Form", *Structure in Art and in Science,* György Kepes (ed.), New York, George Braziller, 1965.

Maki, Fumihiko, and Kawazoe Noboru, *What is Urban Space?,* Tokyo, Tsukuba Publishing Co., 1970.

Fumihiko Maki 1: 1965–78, Contemporary Architects Series, Tokyo, Kajima Publishing Co., 1978.

Maki, Fumihiko, *Visible and Invisible City: A Morphological Analysis of the City of Edo-Tokyo,* Tokyo, Kajima Publishing Co., 1979.

Fumihiko Maki 2: 1979–86, Contemporary Architects Series, Tokyo, Kajima Publishing Co., 1986.

Maki, Fumihiko (and others) *Design Methodology in Technology and Science,* Tokyo, Tokyo University Press, 1987.

Maki, Fumihiko, *Fragmentary Figures: The Collected Architectural Drawings,* Tokyo, Kyuryudo Art Publishing Co. Ltd., 1989.

Maki, Fumihiko, *Memories of Form and Figure: A Collection of Essays on Architecture and Urban Design,* Tokyo, Chikuma Press, 1991.

Maki, Fumihiko, *Details by Maki and Associates: Tepia,* Tokyo, Kajima Publishing Co., 1991.

Maki, Fumihiko, *Kioku No Keisyo: A Collection of Essays,* Tokyo, Kajima Publishing Co., 1992.

Fumihiko Maki 3: 1987–92, Contemporary Architects Series, Tokyo, Kajima Publishing Co., 1993.

Maki, Fumihiko (and others), "A History of Hillside Terrace", Tokyo, Sumai Library Publishing Co., 1995.

Fumihiko Maki: A Presence Called Architecture – Report from the Site, Gallery Ma Books, Catalogue for an exhibition for Gallery Ma, Tokyo, TOTO Shuppan, 1996.

Maki and Associates, *Fumihiko Maki: Buildings and Projects,* New York, Princeton Architectural Press, 1997.

Maki and Associates (eds.), *Stairways of Fumihiko Maki: Details and Spatial Expression,* Tokyo, Shokokusha, 1999 (published in Japanese only).

Fumihiko Maki 4: 1993–99, Contemporary Architects Series, Tokyo, Kajima Publishing Co., 2000.

Maki, Fumihiko, *Selected Passages on the City and Architecture,* internal publication of Maki and Associates, Tokyo, 2000.

Salat, Serge, and Françoise Labbé (eds.), *Fumihiko Maki: An Aesthetic of Fragmentation,* New York, Rizzoli, 1988. (Previously published as *Fumihiko Maki: Une poétique de la fragmentation,* Paris, Electa Moniteur, 1987).

General works

A New Wave of Japanese Architecture: Catalogue 10, New York, The Institute of Architecture and Urban Studies, 1978.

Ashihara, Yoshinobu, *Hidden Orders/Tokyo Through the Twentieth Century.* Tokyo/New York, Kodansha International, 1989.

Banham, Reyner, *Megastructure: Urban Futures of the Recent Past,* New York, Harper and Row, 1976.

Bognar, Botond, *Contemporary Japanese Architecture: Its Development and Challenge,* New York, Van Nostrand Reinhold, 1985.

Bognar, Botond, *Togo Murano: Master Architect of Japan,* New York, Rizzoli, 1996.

Carver, Norman F., *Form and Space of Japanese Architecture,* Tokyo, Shokokusha, 1955.

Chang, Ching-Yu, "Maki, Fumihiko", *Contemporary Architects,* 2nd edition, Chicago and London, St James Press, 1987, p. 506.

de Certeau, Michel, *The Practice of Everyday Life,* Berkeley, University of California Press, 1984.

Engel, Heinrich, *The Japanese House: A Tradition for Contemporary Architecture,* Tokyo, Charles E. Tuttle, 1964.

Fawcett, Chris, *The New Japanese House: Ritual and Anti-ritual: Patterns of Dwelling,* New York, Harper Row, 1980.

Friedman, Mildred (ed.), *Tokyo: Form and Spirit,* Minneapolis, Walker Art Center and New York, Harry N. Abrams Inc., 1986.

Giedion, Sigfried, *Space Time and Architecture,* Cambridge, Mass., Harvard University Press, 1941.

Goodman, Paul and Percival, *Communitas,* Tokyo, Shokokusha, 1967 (translated into Japanese by Fumihiko Maki).

Heidegger, Martin, *Being and Time* (trans. John Macquarie & Edward Robinson), Oxford, Basil Blackwell, 1962.

Hursch, Erhard, *Tokyo,* Tokyo, Charles E. Tuttle, 1965.

Inoue, Mitsuo, *Space in Japanese Architecture* (trans. Hiroshi Watanabe), New York and Tokyo, Weatherhill, 1985.

Kurokawa, Kishio, *New Wave Japanese Architecture,* London, Academy Editions, 1993.

Munroe, A. (ed.), *New Public Architecture: Recent Projects by Fumihiko Maki and Arata Isozaki,* Catalogue for exhibition, New York, Japan Society, 1985.

Ockman, Joan (ed.), *Architecture Culture 1943–1968,* New York, Rizzoli, 1993.

Popham, Peter, *Tokyo: The City at the End of the World,* Tokyo, Kodansha International Ltd., 1985.

Richards, J. M., *An Architectural Journey in Japan,* London, The Architectural Press, 1963.

Ross, Michael Franklin, *Beyond Metabolism: The New Japanese Architecture,* New York, Architectural Record: A McGraw-Hill Publication, 1978.

Rudofsky, Bernard, *Architecture Without Architects: A Short Introduction to Non-pedigreed Architecture,* New York, Museum of Modern Art, 1964.

Scarry, Elaine, *The Body in Pain: The Making and Unmaking of the World,* New York and Oxford, Oxford University Press, 1985.

Shelton Barrie, *Learning from the Japanese City: West Meets East in Urban Design,* London, E & FN Spon, 1999.

Venturi, Robert, *Complexity and Contradiction in Architecture,* New York, Museum of Modern Art, 1966.

Venturi, Robert, Denise Scott Brown, Steven Inezour, *Learning from Las Vegas,* Cambridge, Mass., MIT Press, 1972.

Tokyo Metropolitan Government Publications

Tokyo Fights Pollution: An Urgent Appeal for Reform, Tokyo, Tokyo Metropolitan Government, 1971.

An Administrative Perspective of Tokyo, Tokyo, Tokyo Metropolitan Government, 1975.

City Planning of Tokyo, Tokyo Municipal Government, 1978.

"Tokyo Tomorrow", Tokyo Municipal Library No. 17, 1980.

The 3rd Long-Term Plan for the Tokyo Metropolis (Outline), My Town Tokyo – *For the Dawn of the 21st Century,* Tokyo, Tokyo Municipal Library No. 25, 1991.

The following journals were useful sources of information:

Space Design, The Japan Architect, Progressive Architecture, Architectural Record, Domus, Architecture in Australia, Ekistics, The Architectural Forum, World Architecture, Spazio e Societa, Building.

Of particular interest were the following Special Issues on Fumihiko Maki:

Space Design 6 (177) 1979; *Space Design* 1 (256) 1986; *Space Design* 1 (340) 1993, *Space Design* 1 (424) 2000 and *The Japan Architect* 4 (16) 1994. (The issues of *Space Design* are also cited above under Contemporary Architects Series, Kajima Publishing.)

Illustration Credits

Berthold & Linkersdorff: 59, 84 right, 178 left

Roland Hagenberg: 10

From Inoue, *Space in Japanese Architecture,* Courtesy of Hiroshi Watanabe: 102 left and right

Akio Kawasumi: 74

Toshiharu Kitajima: cover photograph, 30, 31, 32, 53 right, 85, 88, 93 right, 113 left, 115, 116, 118, 121, 126, 141, 142, 157, 159, 164 right, 167, 168 left, 168 top right, 169 right, 173, 174 left, 176 top right, 182, 188, 189

Courtesy of Maki and Associates: 23 top, 42

Maki and Associates: 19, 22, 26, 65 top and bottom, 66, 78, 83 left, 89 left, 100, 101, 105, 146, 187

From *Metabolism: The Proposals for New Urbanism:* 38

From *Movement Systems in the City:* 39, 40, 41 top and bottom

Satora Mishima: 29, 90, 143 (Nikkei Business Publications Inc), 144

Kaneaki Monma: 160 top

Osamu Murai: 60, 61, 109, 124, 158 right, 171, 183 top, 184

From *Notes on Collective Form:* 16

Taisuke Ogawa: 111

Tomio Ohashi: 51, 92

Paul Peck: 123, 174 top right

Shinkenchiku-sha: 79 right, 82, 83 right, 91, 93 left, 113 right, 108, 120 bottom right, 125, 127, 134, 135, 137, 168 bottom right, 169 left, 176 top left, 183 bottom, 185

From *Stairways of Fumihiko Maki: Details and Spatial Expression:* 18

Jennifer Taylor: 49, 79 left, 80, 89 right, 98, 99 top and bottom, 103, 120 bottom left, 162, 166 left, 174 right, 175 top left

Judith Turner: 87, 120 top

Tohru Waki: 77

All other illustrations were provided by Maki and Associates.

Index of Projects